MW01058727

Praise for *Return to Rome*

"This book is an irenic, intimate look at one man's journey of discipleship. But it is much more than that. I have always believed that Protestant/Catholic dialog is important. The two camps must develop awareness and partnership about the things on which they agree, clarity about the things on which they disagree, and charity with discernment about both. This book is sure to advance that dialog. I highly recommend it."

—**J. P. Moreland**, Talbot School of Theology

"A compellingly instructive story of departure and return, loss and recovery, in the Christian's way of discerning the Spirit's lead and responding in the courage of faith."

—**Richard John Neuhaus**, editor in chief, *First Things*

"*Return to Rome* is the story of Frank Beckwith's homecoming. It's a story told without a trace of flippancy or disdain. Frank's love for the faith communities that have shaped his life is obvious; and it gives to his narrative a warmth and a grace that seems to me unique among contemporary conversion stories."

—**Ronald K. Tacelli, SJ**, Boston College

"An interesting, intimate, and intellectually enlightening account of why Francis Beckwith returned to the church of his baptism and his youth. Every good book faces obstacles, and I suspect that this good book will be no different. The denominationally contentious among us will read it, and attack it as Catholic apologetics, as inter-church proselytizing and warfare. It is not. Rather, it's an account, a journey, a story, a memoir, a travelogue. It gives its reasons, to be sure, but it is not apologetics. It's the rich, articulate, and memorable narrative about why one pilgrim decided to go home. Therein lies its value and its contribution."

—**Michael Bauman**, Hillsdale College

"When an Evangelical becomes Catholic, his Protestant acquaintances usually wonder 'How could he do such a thing?' To them it means abandoning the Gospel. In a life story that manages to be charming and erudite at the same time, my friend Frank Beckwith answers the question, showing that taking hold of the Gospel is really what being Catholic is all about. This delightful *apologion* will be not only thought-provoking and informative for Evangelicals trying to decide what to make of their Catholic friends, but wonderfully encouraging for Catholics who aspire to the New Evangelization so often urged by John Paul II."

—**J. Budziszewski**, University of Texas at Austin

"In struggling with the unwelcome appeal of the Catholic Church, Frank Beckwith gave every benefit to the thinking of his Protestant brothers and the long tradition that had formed him for so many years. The result is a careful and generous explanation of the arguments for his entering into full communion with the Catholic Church. His faith memoir will aid mutual understanding between Protestants and Catholics as well as explain why so many serious Evangelicals have found themselves (often unhappily) drawn to Rome."

—**David Mills**, editor,
Touchstone: A Journal of Mere Christianity

Return to ROME

CONFESSIONS of an EVANGELICAL CATHOLIC

Francis J. Beckwith

BrazosPress

a division of Baker Publishing Group
Grand Rapids, Michigan

© 2009 by Francis J. Beckwith

Published by Brazos Press
a division of Baker Publishing Group
P.O. Box 6287, Grand Rapids, MI 49516-6287
www.brazospress.com

Printed in the United States of America

All rights reserved. No part of this publication may be reproduced, stored in a retrieval system, or transmitted in any form or by any means—for example, electronic, photocopy, recording—without the prior written permission of the publisher. The only exception is brief quotations in printed reviews.

Library of Congress Cataloging in Publication Control Number: 2008041845

ISBN 978-1-58743-247-7

Unless otherwise indicated, Scripture is taken from the Catholic Edition of the Revised Standard Version of the Bible, copyright © 1965, 1966 National Council of the Churches of Christ in the United States of America. Used by permission. All rights reserved.

Scripture marked RSV is taken from the Revised Standard Version of the Bible, copyright 1952 [2nd edition, 1971] by the Division of Christian Education of the National Council of the Churches of Christ in the United States of America. Used by permission. All rights reserved worldwide. www.zondervan.com

Scripture marked NIV is taken from the Holy Bible, New International Version®. NIV®. Copyright © 1973, 1978, 1984 by Biblica, Inc.™ Used by permission of Zondervan. All rights reserved worldwide. www.zondervan.com

Scripture marked NKJV is taken from the New King James Version. Copyright © 1982 by Thomas Nelson, Inc. Used by permission. All rights reserved.

Scripture marked NRSV is taken from the New Revised Standard Version of the Bible, copyright © 1989, by the Division of Christian Education of the National Council of the Churches of Christ in the United States of America. Used by permission. All rights reserved.

Scripture marked TNIV is taken from the Holy Bible, Today's New International Version®. TNIV®. Copyright © 2001, 2005 by Biblica Inc.™ Used by permission of Zondervan. All rights reserved worldwide. www.zondervan.com

In keeping with biblical principles of creation stewardship, Baker Publishing Group advocates the responsible use of our natural resources. As a member of the Green Press Initiative, our company uses recycled paper when possible. The text paper of this book is comprised of 30% postconsumer waste.

To my wife, Frankie

Her father, Joseph Alexander Dickerson Jr. (1920–2006), wanted to become Catholic in the late 1940s, but was unable to fulfill his desire. To honor her beloved Daddy, Frankie chose "Joseph" as her Confirmation name when she was received into full communion with the Catholic Church on August 18, 2007, at St. Joseph's Catholic Church, Bellmead, Texas.

Contents

Acknowledgements

I would like to thank my wife, Frankie, and several of our friends and family members who read portions of an earlier version of this book's manuscript: Michael Bauman, Michael Beaty, David Lyle Jeffrey, Katherine Jeffrey, Elizabeth Beckwith Wuebben, Scott Moore, Jonathan Kvanvig, Paul Owen, Scott Hahn, Michael Foley, Jimmy Akin, Myron Steeves, Elizabeth Beckwith, J. Budziszewski, and Ralph Wood. A special thank you to my nephew, Dean Beckwith, for giving me permission to republish my personal letter to him. The book that eventually resulted was the consequence of the brilliant editing of Rodney Clapp of Brazos Press. It was a pleasure to work with both Rodney and Lisa Ann Cockrel. Because of the insights and suggestions I received from all these readers, this is a far better book than it otherwise would have been. However, all of its flaws and shortcomings are mine.

This book would not have been possible if not for the ministry of our pastor, Fr. Timothy Vaverek, the priest that God placed at just the right time and location on the path of our Christian journey. He exemplifies the virtues of the man of God that Paul told Timothy to aim at: "righteousness, godliness, faith, love, steadfastness, gentleness" (1 Tim. 6:11).

A Note on Endnotes

In order for this book to be easy on the eyes, I have placed the notes at the end of the book. Some of these notes contain important comments, citations, references, etc. for those interested in delving deeper into some of the issues discussed in the main text. For example, in chapters 5 and 6 there are notes that deal with aspects of some issues of doctrine and scripture, such as purgatory and prayers for the dead, not addressed directly in the text.

Introduction

> So far as a man may be proud of a religion rooted in
> humility, I am very proud of my religion; I am especially
> proud of those parts of it that are most commonly called
> superstition. I am proud of being fettered by antiquated
> dogmas and enslaved by dead creeds (as my journalistic
> friends repeat with so much pertinacity), for I know very
> well that it is the heretical creeds that are dead, and that
> it is only the reasonable dogma that lives long enough to
> be called antiquated.
>
> G. K. Chesterton, from *The Autobiography of
> G. K. Chesterton* (1936)[1]

It's difficult to explain why one moves from one Christian tradition to another. It is like trying to give an account to your
friends why you chose to pursue marriage to this woman rather
than another, though both may have a variety of qualities that you
found attractive.[2] It seems, then, that any account of my return to
the Catholic Church, however authentic and compelling it is to me,
will appear inadequate to anyone who is convinced I am wrong.
Conversely, my story will confirm in the minds of many devout

11

Catholics that the supernatural power of the grace I received at baptism and confirmation as a youngster were instrumental in drawing me back to Mother Church—after a sojourn of several decades in Evangelical Protestantism. Given these considerations, there is an awkwardness in sharing my journey as a published book, knowing that many fellow Christians will scrutinize and examine my reasons in ways that would appear to some uncharitable and to others too charitable. And I suspect that most of these examiners will see my reasons as mere pretexts for justifying my travel to a destination to which I had unconsciously been moving for quite some time. Nevertheless, given the public nature of my return to the Catholic Church and my former prominence in the world of Evangelical Protestant Christianity, I believe that I have a responsibility, in the words of Peter, "to give an explanation to anyone who asks you for a reason for your hope" (1 Pet. 3:15a).

There are temptations I hope my Catholic and my Protestant Evangelical readers will avoid.

I hope my Catholic readers will resist any temptation to triumphalism. I, of course, believe that Catholicism is in fact true in all its dogmatic theology, including its views of scripture, ethics, church authority, ecumenical councils, etc. I also believe there are many outstanding and persuasive defenses of Catholicism, authored by minds and souls far greater than mine. But my story, because it is a return, requires a departure. And that departure, to be candid, does not speak well of the early post-Vatican II American Church. That Church was littered with dioceses, parishes, and schools that did not adequately catechize their young people with a clear and defensible presentation of the Catholic faith. Things, of course, have changed, and swaths of the American Church seem to be ridding themselves of the vestiges of that unfortunate era. The inspiring pontificates of John Paul II (1978–2005) and Benedict XVI (2005–) have resulted in a new evangelism within the Catholic Church, especially in the United States. Those entering the priesthood seem more serious and theologically orthodox than the priests I remember from the late 1960s and 1970s.

Nevertheless, the American Church lost much as a consequence of those early post-Vatican II days. Its reluctance to properly screen prospective priests for theological fidelity and personal chastity in the deceptively halcyon days of the sexual revolution and its aftermath, coupled with the unchristian company-man instincts of some bishops who reassigned and did not appropriately discipline wayward priests, has brought scandal to the Church in America. This is not to say that the vast majority of priests are not fine Christian men who are honorably and properly administering the sacraments. For this is in fact the case; praise be to God. Rather, it means, to borrow a phrase from Richard Weaver, that ideas have consequences, that what one believes about the nature of theological truth and personal holiness will be cashed out in the catechesis that one prepares and the prospective clergy that one selects and forms.

Not only did some post-Vatican II Catholics and their progeny embrace a secular ethos and abandon their Christian faith entirely, many Catholics, like me, were drawn to Evangelical Protestantism, since it seemed to us that Evangelicals were serious about their faith.[3]

My Evangelical Protestant readers may in my case face a temptation not toward triumphalism, but toward trying to find some subrational reason as to why I returned to the Catholic Church. Several commentators seemed incapable of resisting this temptation during the months following the public announcement of my return. For example, on a May 2007 episode of his radio program, the president of a major Evangelical Protestant seminary discussed my move to Catholicism with one of his school's theologians. During their discussion they spoke kindly and graciously of my academic work and personal character. They are both honorable men for whom I have great respect. At one point in their conversation, however, one of them vocalized his amazement that someone with my intelligence could become Catholic, seeming to imply that Catholicism does not have the intellectual resources a person with real accomplishments, gifts, and theological commitments would find compelling. But that's a road down which no Evangelical Protestant should go, unless he's willing to hold his own theological tradition and its converts and former members to the same level of scrutiny. After all, for every well-known pastor, scholar, or writer who as a young Catholic was drawn to the love of Jesus he or she found in Evangelical Protestant communities, there is a Protestant scholar, pastor or writer who, after years of study and reflection, was compelled to convert to Catholicism.[4]

In July 2007, the Evangelical magazine *Christianity Today* published an editorial that opined about my return to the Roman Catholic Church, noting, "Evangelicals who visit Rome cannot help but enjoy the stately buildings and stirring sense of history. A few like it so much they never leave. Such is the case with Francis Beckwith, former president of the Evangelical Theological Society. In April, the Baylor University philosopher rejoined the Roman Catholic Church." These comments suggest an account of my return that relieves the reader from any obligation to look beyond Vatican City's architectural grandeur and ancient patrimony. One could, of course, turn the tables on this account and draw attention to Evangelical Protestantism's disproportionate number of gaudy mega-church monstrosities that have more in common with Wal-Mart and abandoned warehouses than sacred places of worship. But that would be unfair, for it would amplify one aspect of Evangelical Protestant culture that some may find unattractive, while disregarding those expressions of its ecclesial life that are indeed appealing and draw many to the Christ that is lifted up in such venues. I should say for the record, however, that the only Rome I have ever visited is about 70 miles west of Atlanta. It is, to be sure, a fine city, one that may turn an Auburn Tiger into a Georgia Bulldog, but not a Protestant into a Roman Catholic.

Years ago, while I was studying for my PhD, Augustine's *Confessions* had a profound impact on me. It showed me how faith and reason were not incommensurable categories that reside in the same soul side by side while never touching. Rather, they are natural human faculties designed by God for our acquisition of knowledge. When ordered to the right end, they work together in cooperation for the good of the whole person. As Augustine put it, "I believe, in order to understand; and I understand, the better to believe."[5]

And yet, as a Christian philosopher, whether Protestant or Catholic, I must also take into account a third temptation, warned against by Paul in Colossians 2:8–9: "Beware lest any man spoil you through philosophy and vain deceit, after the tradition of men, after the rudiments of the world, and not after Christ" (KJV). This passage reminds me of how important it is for one to remain true to the Gospel and to be diligent in recognizing the alluring temptation of being impressed by, and for that reason, more easily deceived by, one's own philosophical speculations and professional accomplishments.

It would be a mistake, however, to read Colossians 2:8–9 as a warning against the study of philosophy. This passage is no more telling Christians to stay away from philosophy than a command not to drink poison is telling Christians to avoid all study of pharmacy. Just as one cannot tell the difference between arsenic and medicine without knowing something about pharmacology, one cannot discern the difference between bad and good philosophy or sound and unsound reasoning, without an adequate grasp of philosophical and logical principles. Paul's example at the Aeropagus (Acts 17:16–32) shows us why Christians should take seriously the advice of C. S. Lewis: "To be ignorant and simple now–not to be able to meet the enemies on their own ground–would be to throw down our weapons, and to betray our uneducated brethren who have, under God, no defence but us against the intellectual attacks of the heathen. *Good philosophy must exist, if for no other reason, because bad philosophy needs to be answered*" (emphasis mine).[6] My mission as a Christian philosopher—both as a Protestant and a Catholic—has been, and continues to be, driven by Lewis's important insight.

With these three temptations observed, I can say more precisely what it is I intend this book to be. What I hope to offer here is an account of a personal journey that focuses on my own internal conversation, or struggle, between the Protestant theology I embraced during most of my adult life and what I've come to think of as my Catholic constitution, which I have to believe had always been there. Much of this book is a celebration of the Christianity that has shaped my life, intellectually and spiritually, both in its Protestant and Catholic forms. I do indeed explain how and why my mind changed, but with respect and admiration for the Evangelical

Protestants whom the Holy Spirit used to deepen my devotion to Christ, which I carry with gratitude into the Catholic Church. Thus, this book is a narrative intertwined with encounters, arguments, criticisms, and reflections. It is not meant to be an apologetic for Catholicism or an autobiography in the strict sense.

It is my hope that this book may effectively, with grace and charity, communicate to my fellow Christians, both Protestant and Catholic, an understanding of the reasons and internal deliberations that culminated in my departure from and eventual return to the Catholic Church.

1

Confession on the Brazos

For Thou hast made us for Thyself, and our hearts are
restless until they rest in Thee.

St. Augustine, from *The Confessions* (c. 398 AD)[1]

I
t was a spring Texas afternoon, a little hot, not too humid. I had
arrived at St. Jerome's Catholic Church. St. Jerome's is located
in Waco, Texas, the home of my employer, Baylor University—
sometimes called "Jerusalem on the Brazos." Although the church
is only about three miles from my home in the adjacent town of
Woodway, my arrival on that April 28, 2007 afternoon marked a
turning point in a long spiritual pilgrimage that began in 1973 in
Las Vegas, Nevada. I had come to church that Saturday to receive
the sacrament of reconciliation, which to many is known as confession. This ordinarily would not be such a big deal, except that it was
my first confession in more than 30 years. And at the completion
of the sacrament I would be in full communion with the Catholic
Church. My younger brother James emailed me earlier in the week
and had jokingly asked if I needed help in recalling my sins.

Of course, people become Catholic every day. But in my case, I knew that there would be ramifications: I was the president of the Evangelical Theological Society (ETS), an academic society with nearly 4500 members. I was also a fairly well-known public intellectual who had gone through a very public tenure battle at Baylor University that had, fortunately, ended in my favor only seven months earlier.[2]

Upon entering the confessional, I sat face-to-face with the priest. I said, "Father, forgive me, for I have sinned. It has been over 30 years since my last confession." Then I said, "I'm not sure I can remember all of my sins." In his thick East Indian accent, he replied, "That is all right. God knows them all." I responded, "I was afraid of that." The priest then heard my confession and granted me absolution. I found my way to the main sanctuary, where I did my penance, which consisted of one "Our Father" and one "Hail Mary." When I told this to my wife, Frankie, she thought the priest was far too lenient. She has a thorough recollection of my sins.

During the last week of March 2007, after much prayer, counsel, and consideration, my wife and I decided to seek full communion with the Catholic Church. Given my status in ETS, I had decided—after consultation with trusted friends—not to seek to return to the Church until my term as ETS president had ended in November 2007. I would then permanently resign from the ETS executive committee. (Former presidents may be committee members for four years following their presidential terms.) I wanted to make sure that my return to the Catholic Church brought as little attention to ETS as possible. To complicate matters, I received conflicting advice from wise friends regarding how and when to address the ETS executive committee on this delicate matter. Some suggested the committee would rather not know about my reception into the Church until after the national meeting in November. These friends recommended I lie low, give a presidential address that was irenic and did not address Protestant-Catholic issues (which I had planned on doing all along), and then quietly ask not to be nominated to the executive committee for the four-year, at-large term.

Other friends, equally as wise, opined that by withholding from the executive committee my plans to return to the Church, I would play to prejudices that some Protestants have about "secretive Jesuit conspiracies" and the like.

Prayerful Confirmation

I did not know what to do. Frankie and I prayed and asked the Lord to provide us with clear direction. We believe we received this direction on the morning of April 20. Frankie and I were visiting in Washington, DC, having breakfast with my parents. My cell phone rang, interrupting our breakfast. It was my sixteen-year-old nephew, Dean Beckwith. Dean called to ask if I would be his sponsor when he received the sacrament of Confirmation on May 13. Several months earlier I had written a letter to Dean, at the behest of his mother. She had asked several of us, including his other aunts and uncles, to write a note to Dean explaining the importance of affirming his Christian baptism at confirmation. This is what I had written to him in a letter dated March 6, 2007:

> *Dear Dean:*
>
> *I'm writing to offer you my encouragement as you partake in the sacrament of confirmation. I am sure you were taught much in your catechism about the meaning of confirmation and its significance in affirming in public your commitment to the Gospel of Jesus Christ and your desire to be one of our Lord's followers. . . . I want to focus in this letter of encouragement on the spiritual and intellectual tradition in which you find yourself. It is a tradition that includes some of the wisest, smartest, holiest, and influential minds in the history of humanity. To quote the author of Hebrews, "we are surrounded by so great a cloud of witnesses . . ." (Heb. 12:1).*
>
> *Let us begin at the beginning. Jesus of Nazareth is the smartest and wisest man who ever lived. No one can compare with his insights, his deft combination of love, tenderness, tough-mindedness, and mercy. His life and his ideas reshaped*

the ancient world and changed the trajectory of history itself.
You are one of his followers. What an amazing privilege.

Either Jesus was who he said he was—the Son of God—or
he was a liar, or he was a lunatic [as C. S. Lewis once put it].
These are the only options. Yet, the picture of Jesus that we
receive is one of a psychologically balanced individual who
had incredible wisdom concerning our duties to others and
our relationship to God. He was willing to die, which means
he believed himself to be who he said he was. . . . A liar may
do many things, but he does not march to his death for what
he knows to be false. Thus, Jesus was either a lunatic—he
sincerely believed himself to be the Son of God even though
he was not—or he was Lord—he sincerely believed himself
to be the Son of God because he was the Son of God. As
the Cambridge scholar C. S. Lewis has pointed out, many
people believe that Jesus was a great moral teacher. But if he
was, it is unlikely that he was a lunatic. Great moral teachers
are typically balanced, mature people possessing intestinal
fortitude and personal integrity. Do you think the picture
of Jesus we get from history and the New Testament is that
of a lunatic, a David Koresh or Osama Bin Laden, bent on
a single idea that is self-defeating? It does not seem that
way to me. It seems to me that Jesus was neither a liar nor a
lunatic. But that means that he was Lord. Those are the only
options. I know that you confess Jesus as Lord. But it's always
good to remind ourselves about Jesus and why he stands
out in history and why we measure history by his birth.

There are certain core-facts about Jesus's death that
virtually all scholars agree on: (1) Jesus died by crucifixion;
(2) His tomb was found empty three days later; (3) His
followers (the apostles and other disciples) believed that
they had had experiences with Christ after his death; (4) His
followers were willing to suffer death for their belief that
they had met the risen Christ. These facts, which are not
even disputed by most unbelieving scholars, are difficult to
account for apart from Jesus actually rising from the dead.

Although it is common for those who doubt the resurrection to say that the early church made up the story, this theory fails to account for the church itself (not to mention having no evidence in its favor). That is, Jesus's resurrection makes sense as the cause of the early church, a body of believers who personally knew Jesus and would have recanted their belief if they knew that the resurrection was a fabrication. But not one of Jesus's early disciples who believed that they had met Jesus after the resurrection ever recanted. In fact, many of them (including 11 of the 12 apostles) suffered horrible torture and death for their beliefs, something that does not make sense if they had made up the whole thing. Granted, people die for false beliefs. But rarely if ever does anyone die for a belief they know is false. These are some of the earliest witnesses that form the cloud that surrounds us.

Under the leadership of St. Peter and St. Paul, the church grew from a small band of believers to an international phenomenon that through its message slowly but eventually dismantled the spiritual infrastructure of the greatest empire the world had ever known, the Roman Empire. As the church moved through history, it began to reflect on its own theology and produce some of the clearest creeds ever penned, such as the Apostles' Creed and the Nicene Creed. But that is not all. The church's finest minds were willing to wrestle with and respond to the non-Christian challenges of their day, to follow St. Paul's instruction to take "every thought captive to the obedience of Christ" (2 Cor. 10:5). Throughout church history, and even to this present day, gifted Christians became well versed in the philosophy, literature, sciences, and arts of their day. For they believed, as we all should believe, that all truth is God's truth, that the Christian worldview illuminates our understanding of the world and the order and nature of things. The enormity of Christian influence in the shaping of Western civilization boggles the mind. Ideas about human nature, economics, the sciences, the arts, ethics, architecture, music, mathematics, and politics flourished under the direction of Christian intellectuals and leaders. According to my Baylor colleague, Professor Rodney Stark (in his book For the Glory of God *[Princeton University Press, 2002]), without Christianity's understanding of God and nature, much of what we take for granted today—including our legal system, our understanding of truth, and the success of the sciences—would have never come to be.*

You, indeed we, stand on the shoulders of predecessors whose beliefs about God, man, and nature—derived explicitly from their Christian faith—furnished the cultural infrastructure that gave rise to the knowledge, wealth, and liberties that make it possible for us today to freely worship God and to study his world.

The Lord has given you many gifts. Use them wisely. But do not ever forget that you now stand with that great cloud of witnesses.

It should be evident that I could not say "no" to my dear nephew, who had credited the renewal of his faith in Christ to our conversations and this correspondence. But in order for me to be his confirmation sponsor I would have to be in full communion with the Catholic Church. Because I had received the sacraments of Baptism, Communion, and Confirmation all before the age of fourteen, I needed only to go to confession, request forgiveness for my sins, ask to be received back into the Church, and receive absolution. And that is what I did on that spring day in Texas, April 28, 2007. The next day I was publicly received back into the Catholic Church at the 11:00 a.m. Mass at St. Joseph's Catholic Church in Bellmead, Texas. My wife, standing beside me, was accepted as a candidate for full communion. She was received into the Church on August 18, 2007, at the culmination of her catechesis.

My Christian Vocation

Prior to my return to the Church, virtually all of my professional work in Christian philosophy and apologetics, as well as in legal, political, and moral philosophy, has focused on questions and issues of concern to all Christians, regardless of theological or ecclesiastical tradition. For example, long before I had thought about returning to the Catholic Church, I had written about and defended the Catholic Church's positions on abortion, natural theology, and the natural moral law—positions held by many other non-Catholic Christians as well. The manuscript for my book, *Defending Life: A Moral and Legal Case Against Abortion Choice*, was written while I was a committed Protestant, though the publisher, Cambridge University Press, released it after I had returned to the Catholic Church. And yet, there's nothing in *Defending Life* that a pro-life Catholic or Protestant would find inconsistent with his or her theological tradition. So, I do not anticipate my return to the Church radically altering the sort of work that I have been doing for years, and which has been well-received by Catholic and non-Catholic Christians alike.

In 2004 I coedited a book with my good friends J. P. Moreland and William Lane Craig, *To Everyone An Answer: A Case for the Christian Worldview*.[3] It was a volume in honor of our mentor and friend, Norman L. Geisler, a self-described "Evangelical Thomist." (A "Thomist" is a follower of the great philosopher and theologian, Thomas Aquinas [1225–74].) I authored the book's introduction, which includes the following description of the *Christian Worldview* (notes omitted):

> What do we mean when we say that Christianity is a *worldview*? What we mean is that the Christian faith is a philosophical tapestry of interdependent ideas, principles, and metaphysical claims that are derived from the Hebrew-Christian Scriptures as well as the creeds, theologies, communities, ethical norms, and institutions that have flourished under the authority of these writings. These beliefs are not mere utterances of private religious devotion, but are propositions whose proponents claim accurately instruct us on the nature of the universe, human persons, our relationship with God, human communities, and the moral life. The following is a summary of some of these beliefs.
>
> First, there exists an eternally self-existing moral agent named God, who created the universe ex nihilo. The universe is completely

and absolutely contingent upon God for its beginning as well as its continued existence. He is, among other things, personal, omnipotent, omniscient, omnipresent, perfectly good, necessary, and infinitely wise. . . .

Second, God created human beings in his image. A human being is not merely a collection of physical parts but has an underlying unity or soul. A human being's life is sacred from the moment that human being comes into existence; the value of a human being is not something acquired when he or she reaches a certain level of physical complexity, as many secular thinkers maintain. Because human beings are moral agents, they have the capacity to make decisions and judgments within the larger framework of family and community. Thus, for the Christian worldview, marriage, government, and church are not merely social constructions that can be shaped in any way consistent with some utopian vision of justice, but rather, are natural institutions in which and by which human beings ought to learn what is good, true, and beautiful. . . .

Third, God reveals himself both in special revelation (2 Tim. 3:14–17), the Bible, as well as general revelation. Concerning the former, if the Bible is truly God's word, then it must be inerrant, for God himself is perfect (Mark 10:18; Heb. 6:18), and it follows logically that his Word must be as well. The Bible provides us with (1) an account of humanity's genesis and fall, (2) a history of God's chosen people, (3) the institution of the law of Moses and its inadequacy to redeem, (4) prophecy, prayer, wisdom and poetry, and (5) the good news and story of the first coming of the Messiah and the establishing of his church on earth.

The latter is the cornerstone of Christian faith. According to the Bible, human beings have violated the moral law of God and need to be made right with Him. That is, human beings are in need of salvation but are powerless to achieve this on their own. This is why God became a human being in Jesus of Nazareth so that he may pay the sacrifice necessary to atone for our sins, his own death on the cross. Christians believe that Jesus rose bodily from the grave three days after his death and 40 days later ascended into heaven. Shortly after that Jesus's apostles and disciples established His church, a body of believers that continues to grow to this very day. . . .

According to scripture, God has not left himself without a witness among the unbelievers (Acts 14:17). This is called general revelation, since it is something that all people have the capacity to access through observation, reason, and reflection apart from the Bible. [4]

At the time I published the above in 2004, I was a firmly committed Evangelical Protestant. Yet, there is nothing in these paragraphs that I do not believe as a Catholic. Of course, Catholicism commits me to a richer or more detailed array of theological beliefs than what I presented above. But that fact does not diminish these beliefs. This is why it does not seem peculiar to me to think of myself as both Evangelical and Catholic, though I am fully aware that some have and will continue to dispute this self-understanding.

Yet, if one is a careful reader with an eye for detecting an underlying idea that accounts for a text's apparent continuity, one will have noticed, as I noticed only later, that both my letter to Dean as well as my introductory comments from *To Everyone An Answer* presuppose the Church, that irreducible living substance, the Body of Christ, that remains identical to itself as it marches through history. This Church plays an integral part in the formation and fixation of Christian doctrine and scripture as well as our understanding of how the Christian faith illuminates and enhances our knowledge of every aspect of life including the academic disciplines. But, of course, accepting such an understanding of ecclesiology, theology, and the biblical canon does not make one a Catholic, even though it is consistent with Catholic dogmatic and moral theology. How then did I come to leave Catholicism, think of myself as Protestant, and then return to the Church more than three decades later? That will be the focus of the next four chapters.

2

Viva Las Vegas

Running a casino is like robbing a bank with no cops
around. For guys like me, Las Vegas washes away your
sins. It's like a morality car wash.

Sam "Ace" Rothstein,
character in the movie, *Casino* (1995)

I was born in 1960 in Brooklyn, New York. My mother, Elizabeth
Guido, also born in Brooklyn, is Italian-American. Her four
grandparents were several of the many Italian-Catholic immigrants
that passed through Ellis Island in the late-nineteenth century and
the early twentieth century. My father, Harold Beckwith, was born
in Connecticut. His mother was a French-Canadian Catholic. His
father was of English descent and a baptized Episcopalian. I'm the
eldest of my parents' four children.

What Happens in Vegas . . .

In January 1967, my immediate family at the time—Mom, Dad,
and younger brother James—moved to Las Vegas, Nevada. There

my father worked as an accountant and internal auditor at a number of hotels, including The Dunes, Caesar's Palace, The Thunderbird, The Four Queens, The Fremont, The Stardust, and The Aladdin. We initially came to Vegas when my father agreed to be the accountant for, and a partner with, my uncle and others in a business called Gelo's Lounge, a Chinese restaurant and bar. My Uncle Fiore "Jimmy" Casella, who died of a drug overdose in 1976, was a well-known professional gambler, having earned the Seven Card Razz and Seven Card Stud world championships at the 1974 World Series of Poker. He was a colorful character who looked a lot like Phil Foster, the actor who played the father of the character Laverne De Fazio (Penny Marshall) in the TV sitcom "Laverne & Shirley." According to Frank Marino, who claims to have dealt cards to my Uncle Fiore during his heyday: "Sarge [another card player] and Jimmy Casella were just outright mean and supposedly connected. To quote one of my favorite poker personalities, Chicken Man Cantrell, 'You mess with them, you're likely to wake up with a groundhog for a mailman.' "[1]

Needless to say, my Uncle Fiore was not a practicing Catholic or Christian of any sort. However, his wife, my Aunt Doris, became a committed Christian a few years after her husband's 1976 death, though she never returned to the Catholic Church of her Baptism. Several of their children have had born-again experiences. Among them was their second eldest son, Peter, who became a Pentecostal pastor for a short time in the 1980s after his remarkable transformation from pimp and drug abuser to outspoken Christian. Peter and his girlfriend (and future wife) answered an altar call to receive Christ at a 1979 Leon Patillo concert performed at the University of Nevada, Las Vegas.

At that same concert Patillo told the audience after the altar call that several months earlier Bob Dylan had become a Christian. I had been a fan of Dylan's music for over a year when I heard Patillo's announcement. In fact, in November 1979, I joined Peter, Ruth (Peter's wife), and Peter's younger brother, Fiore Jr., in attending a Dylan concert in San Francisco, in which Dylan performed only songs from his overtly Christian album, *Slow Train Coming* (1979), and his forthcoming collection, *Saved* (1980). It was an amazing experience. I had never been to a "Christian" concert in which half the audience was praising the Lord while the other half was smoking pot, though I suspect there were some audience members who were doing both. As the concert went into its encore portions, many of Dylan's fans who had hoped to hear a Dylan classic, like "Blowin' in the Wind" or "Like a Rolling Stone," realized, to their dismay, that it was not going to happen that evening. Some began to boo and yell obscenities at him, while others walked out in disgust, demanding their money back. Seemingly to issue a stern reply to this spectacle that was occurring in front of him, Dylan, sitting at the piano, began singing "Pressing On."

Accompanied by only four female Gospel singers, his piano issuing slow rhythm and blues riffs, Dylan belted out his words as if he were a prophet who had just returned from the wilderness with a divine warning to stir the wayward masses. Peter, Ruth, Fiore, and I stood, cried, and clapped in awe at this cacophony of sounds, smells, voices, and words that were transcended by the clarity of the Christian message emanating from Bob Dylan's microphone. That was an experience that has stuck with me for decades.[2]

Although I rejoice in the conversions of these relatives, the consequences of how my Aunt and Uncle conducted their lives while bringing up their children have rippled through the generations with sad results. Some of their children and grandchildren have done better than others, and some of them are presently doing quite well and seem to have reasonably normal family lives. But when one's character has been shaped by a Vegas culture of unbridled indulgence, combined with parents living disordered lives, it is only with great difficulty that one can reorient oneself away from such deeply embedded influences. Looking back at what has been wrought in this branch of my family has helped make me more confident in the teachings of the Catholic Church on marriage, family, and the common good.

Thankfully, my parents kept my siblings and me pretty much in the dark about the scandalous details of the Casella side of our family. My parents did not smoke, only occasionally imbibed alcohol, put us through Catholic schools for twelve years, and took us to Mass every Sunday. Like me, all of my siblings received the sacraments of Baptism, Holy Communion, and Confirmation. We lived pretty standard American Catholic lives for the era, with Vegas and its culture being incidental to our home life and our relationship with our parents. However, my parents were, and are, instinctively charitable people, revealing something from the Church and its teachings that had been placed deeply in their hearts. For example, whenever one of the Casellas needed a place to stay, my parents took them in, oftentimes for a few days, sometimes for months and even years! My parents treated my cousins as if they were their own sons, and none of us ever felt deprived for that. In fact, I'm confident that my parents' spirit of generosity enhanced, rather than diminished, the love we had for one another. For this reason, some in the family would on occasion jokingly refer to our home as "Boys Town."

We always seemed to have guests over for Sunday dinner, which consisted of my Sicilian mother's pasta and meatballs. These dinner guests ranged from friends and relatives to the friends and acquaintances of friends and relatives. Guests were entertained by (or forced to hear, depending on one's sense of humor) my father and his many jokes and stories. A Korean War Veteran, my father had done some emceeing and stand-up comedy while serving in the U.S. Army. Whatever comedic skills he acquired while working for Uncle Sam, they were not missing in action when he returned to the states. It made our home a wonderful place in which to grow up.

My parents exposed me to the importance of politics and citizenship at an early age. In the mid-1960s, they encouraged my brother James and me to watch important political events and speeches. In 1968, when I was seven years old, I distinctly remember watching and listening to Senator Robert F. Kennedy on the evening he was assassinated in Los Angeles, and seeing my parents cry when his death was announced on our television hours later. Only months earlier, Martin Luther King Jr. had been murdered in Memphis. My parents supported the Civil Rights Movement and were diligent in making sure that my brother and I knew of Dr. King and the tragedy of his death. Although I was too young to remember the presidency of John F. Kennedy, my father made sure we listened to the late president's 1961 inaugural address, one of the great political speeches in American history. On several occasions, my father played the recording of Kennedy's speech on our old family turntable. As in other matters, my father also had a sense of humor about politics. When I was eight years old I asked him to explain to me the difference between communism and capitalism. He answered, "Well, son, in America, a capitalist country, some people own Cadillacs and some people don't. But in communist countries like the Soviet Union, everyone is treated equally, and no one owns a Cadillac."

During several months in my middle school years I would return home every afternoon to see my mother watching the Watergate Hearings, chaired by one of her heroes, Senator Sam Ervin. She always invited me to join her, which I usually did. I was fascinated by the hearings, the issues surrounding them, and the historical importance of all the figures that were participating. As I grew older and began to develop my own political opinions, my parents exhibited a level of tolerance and openness that was exemplary. While my father and I became more conservative in our views over the years, my mother remained a moderate Democrat (as she is today). However, my conservatism, ironically, developed out of my liberalism. I was taught by my parents that one of the roles of government was to protect the "little guy" and to make sure that those not well off should be given a chance to succeed and make a decent living. But in my early twenties I began to notice that self-described liberals had no interest in protecting the littlest guy of all, the unborn, and that they often advanced policies that inhibited economic growth, and thus harmed those who most needed the wealth produced by free markets, the poor and the underprivileged. So, for me, true liberalism is conservative, for it strives to protect and nurture, indeed conserve, those people, institutions, and practices that advance the common good and thus provide a framework for human flourishing.

I have so many fond memories of growing up. One in particular left an indelible mark. In the summer of 1972 I played the position of catcher on a Little League baseball team. Although I was a pretty good defensive player, I was a terrible hitter. My parents knew this, since they attended my games and heard me complain about my numerous strikeouts. In order to remedy this, my parents went into action. My mother—a voracious reader—bought me a book on hitting authored by the great Boston Red Sox player, Ted Williams. My father sat me down and told me that we would both read the book and then after completing it, spend two hours every night for a week at the local batting cages, putting Williams's lessons into action. We read the book and went to the cages. My father meticulously went over Williams's lessons, and he did so with great patience, for I was given to emotional outbursts if I did not succeed the first time I faced the mechanical pitcher.[3] In the face of such tantrums, my father employed his disarming sense of humor while he remained encouraging and yet determined. By the end of the week, I was easily hitting sixty-mile-per-hour fastballs. I was ready.

At the next Little League game, I had my chance. The bases were loaded. We were down by two runs, and it was the bottom of the last inning. At my turn to bat, I swung and hit a line drive that was bounding over the third baseman's head. He jumped as high as he could, and with perfect timing caught the ball at the tip of his glove. The game ended, and we lost. Although I was disappointed in losing, for the first time that season I actually hit the ball hard and with confidence, and, in this case, nearly won the game for my team. For the rest of the season my batting average hovered around .400, and I had become a legitimate offensive threat. The next season I had the second highest batting average on the team. What I learned from my parents was the importance of doing things well and doing so patiently and carefully with deliberate determination.

Property of Jesus

I was baptized Catholic as an infant and received the sacrament of confirmation when I was in seventh grade in May 1973. It was soon after my confirmation that I became fascinated by the person of Jesus and wanted to know more about this incredible man. It all began one evening in October 1973, several days before my thirteenth birthday. I went to sleep that night and had the most vivid dream of Jesus and me. We were sitting, facing each other, with the landscape of heaven in the background. He spoke to me. Over thirty years later, I cannot honestly recall the words he uttered. But I do remember waking up the next morning with the sense that I had experienced a reality that was unlike any dream I had ever had. Coincidentally, that evening my father was visited by a friend of his, who was sharing with my father his own spiritual journey that led him to become deeply embedded in the Catholic Charismatic movement. On our kitchen table, this friend had left for my father a copy of a *Good News for Modern Man New Testament* (Today's English Version). The following afternoon I picked it up and began reading it. I had no idea, until days later, that I had been reading a Bible. I initially thought it was just some religious book about Jesus. I was so taken by the person of Christ I found in the Gospels that only days into my reading about this marvelous man, I actually tried to live out Jesus's commandments in the playground and in the classroom. I recall one incident in which a bully at school punched me during recess. I literally turned the other cheek and offered it to him for a second punch. He freaked out, walked away, and told me I was weird. The other students did not really know what to make of me.

The next time my father's friend visited our home I worked up the nerve to ask him about the book and his faith. He invited me to a small Jesus People church in downtown Las Vegas, Maranatha House. Run by hippies who had become enthusiastic Christians (this was, after all, the mid-1970s), Maranatha House offered to many of us a place where we learned scripture, heard dynamic teachings, sang freely of our faith, and were introduced to books and tapes by a variety of writers and speakers who seemed to have real insight into theological matters. Some of the earliest folks I read and listened to included the "Bible Answer Man" Walter R. Martin, Lutheran theologian John Warwick Montgomery (whom I would later study under for my first graduate degree), Pentecostal evangelist David Wilkerson, Chinese missionary and mystic Watchman Nee, Calvary Chapel founder Chuck Smith, and dispensationalists Hal Lindsey and Salem Kirban, both of whom were precursors to the "Left Behind" book craze. It seemed to me that the people at

Maranatha House were serious about their commitment to Christ. Except for my experience in the Catholic Charismatic Movement soon after visiting Maranatha House, I had seen nothing like it in the Catholic Church.

With all these new experiences and theological ideas, along with continued Bible reading, I became somewhat of a religious know-it-all around my family and schoolmates. A 1973 incident stands out. My Dad's older brother, Russell (my baptismal godfather), and his wife, Patricia, were visiting our home for dinner. During dessert and coffee, my Uncle Russ and Aunt Pat were talking with my parents about how certain white employees at the Nevada Test Site (where my uncle worked as a security guard) were being passed over for promotion and that black employees, who had far less seniority than their white colleagues, were being promoted. My uncle and aunt were very upset about this, since it seemed to them to be unfair and unjust. Overhearing the discussion, I walked into the kitchen with Bible in hand, sat at the table, and opened up the scriptures to those passages that condemn racism and class distinctions among Christians (e.g., Gal. 3:26–29). As if to show off my growing knowledge of the Bible, I then began quoting passages I thought my aunt and uncle ought to hear, implying that they were harboring unbiblical attitudes toward the black employees at the test site. I must have come across as a real self-righteous jackass, as evidenced by the mildly amused looks on my parents' faces and my uncle's unwillingness to immediately acquiesce to the biblical proof-texting of this precocious though presumptuous thirteen-year-old.

Leaving the Catholic Church

Because I was born in 1960, I was part of the first generation of American Catholics who would have no memory of the Church prior to Vatican II. This also meant that I grew up, and attended Catholic schools, during a time in which well-meaning Catholic leaders were testing all sorts of innovations in the church, many of which were deleterious to the proper formation of young people. Vatican II itself was not the problem. The problem was the implementation of its reforms and the way in which some Catholics misinterpreted its documents due to the influence of widely held cultural views that were in some ways antithetical to a mature Christian faith.

In my parents' parish, St. Viator Catholic Church, Masses were often peppered with contemporary songs such as "Bridge Over Troubled Water," "I Don't Know How to Love Him" (from *Jesus Christ Superstar*), as well as popular folk songs including the dreaded "Kumbaya" and "Michael, Row the Boat Ashore." Some of the Masses had an informal quality to them that I'm sure seemed more accessible to many Catholics who had a pre-Vatican II experience. But, as I reflect back on those days and what I know now, it seems that something sacred was taken away from God's people, though I'm sure no one intended such a consequence. The way Mass was conducted in many parishes seemed to trivialize the liturgy of the Eucharist in such a way that its significance was diminished. Some parishes removed their kneelers, crucifixes, and statues. Newly built church buildings were constructed with modernist architectural designs. Thus, when you walked into some churches, you had an immediate sense of minimalism and spiritual barrenness, and not the majesty of God. The Blessed Sacrament was nowhere to be found. And if you were lucky, there would be a confessional, but it was rarely used. At most of these parishes, some of which were made up of thousands of families, the sacrament of confession (or reconciliation) was offered "by appointment only." (I've always wondered how one makes an appointment for a confession that allows the penitent to remain anonymous. One can only imagine it may go something like this. With a badly disguised voice, the future penitent inquires: "I'd like to make an appointment for confession. I'll be waiting in the back of the church with a hood and sunglasses.")

I served as an altar boy at scores of these Masses, until the end of my 8th grade year. Some of the priests who celebrated them seemed to be annoyed at liturgical innovations, though others seemed to embrace them. As I reflect on those times, it now seems as if the priests who did not like these changes felt helpless to resist the cultural tsunami that appeared to have overtaken their Church. Many of them were elderly and nearing retirement. The younger priests were enthusiastic about the changes, and it seemed as if the parishioners were embracing them without much of a fuss. There were, of course, pockets of public resistance throughout American Catholicism. But you wouldn't know it from my parish and the catechesis it offered in its elementary school.

The traditional Filipino nuns who had run the school since its inception, and always wore full habits with giant rosaries attached, were replaced in 1971 by American nuns who dressed in secular outfits. The new principal wore knee-length, form-fitting skirts and snug blouses that accentuated her attractive figure. For a sixth grade boy, this image did not bring to mind "consecrated virgin." Needless to say, I had a crush on her, even though she had a face for radio. This led to several bad habits, so to speak.

My religion teachers often spoke of Catholicism as "our tradition" rather than as a cluster of beliefs that were true. This relativizing of the faith did not engender confidence in the young students under their tutelage. Moreover, basic Catholic doctrine was often presented inadequately. One day, for example, when discussing the issues of sin and salvation, one teacher told us that when you die and meet God, he weighs your sins and good deeds on a scale, and if the latter outweighs the former, one avoids eternal damnation. And because one did not behave perfectly, one had to spend time in purgatory, a place that is like Hell insofar as it is not pleasant. But it is also unlike Hell because it ends. That same teacher used the following illustration to explain the difference between these two posthumous fates: in Hell, there is a clock on the wall and it never stops; but in purgatory, there is also a clock on the wall and it does stop. None of this, of course, is Catholic theology. It was as if this teacher had learned about Catholic theology from Protestant fundamentalist evangelistic tracts rather than from the works of her own theologians.

On the other hand, there were some very important renewal movements in the Church at the time. The Catholic Charismatic Movement had a profound impact on me. During my middle school years, while attending Maranatha House, I also frequented a Catholic Charismatic Bible study led by friends of my parents. Some of the folks at that Bible study were instrumental in bringing to my parents' parish three Dominican priests who offered a weeklong evening seminar on the Bible and the Christian life. I attended that seminar and was very much taken by the Dominicans' erudition and deep spirituality, as well as the love of Jesus that was evident in the way they conducted themselves. I recall peppering one of them with all sorts of theological questions, and he was more than happy to provide cogent and clear answers. When I began quoting scripture to him, in order to defend my Protestant-leaning beliefs, he wisely told me that biblical passages must be read in their context and not used to proof-text one's pet doctrines. As an example, he quoted to me from Psalm 14, "There is no God," and said, "You see, Frank, the Bible teaches atheism." Seeing the quizzical look on my face, he went on to say, "What you have to look at is the context, which is 'The fool says in his heart, "There is no God." They are corrupt, they do abominable deeds, there is none that does good. The LORD looks down from heaven upon the children of men, to see if there are any that act wisely, that seek after God'" (Ps. 14:1–2). I have always looked back fondly on that encounter, and I am grateful for that priest's willingness to take the time to teach me an important lesson.

As a young Catholic male, I naturally began thinking that maybe I was being called to the priesthood. Because I wasn't sure what to do, I prayed and asked God to provide me a clear indication of whether he wanted me to pursue the sacrament of Holy Orders. As fate would have it, puberty soon kicked in and thoughts of lifetime celibacy vanished as quickly as my clear complexion. On a more serious note, I still wonder what would have happened if a local priest or devout Catholic layman had taken notice of my theological exploration and offered me guidance. Perhaps such a scenario was never in the divine cards (that's my Vegas background talking), and I wound up exactly where I was supposed to wind up. I'll never know on this side of eternity. But what I do know is that I cannot imagine my life without my dear wife, Frankie, who is a true gift of God.

To be sure, I had many positive experiences within the Catholic Church. But I was much more impressed with the commitment to following Christ as well as the personal warmth and high view of scripture that I found among the Protestants with which I had interacted at Maranatha House and other local congregations. Looking back, I believe that the Catholic Church's weakness was presenting the renewal movements like the charismatic movement as something new and not part of the Church's theological traditions. For someone like me, interested in both the spiritual and intellectual grounding of the Christian faith, I didn't need the "folk Mass" with cute nuns and hip priests playing "Kumbaya" with guitars, tambourines, and harmonicas. And it was usually not done very well, if my experiences and those of many of my friends and scores of my contemporaries with whom I have spoken and corresponded are correct. Combine that with a watered-down and intellectually vapid presentation of the Gospel, and is it any wonder that many of us made a mad dash to where we saw Christ lifted up in Evangelical Protestantism? Instead of playing to its strengths—historical continuity with the early church, theological sophistication, a high view of scripture, a true counter-cultural understanding of the human person and social justice, and profound and life changing spiritual practices and traditions—the American Church offered to the young people of my day lousy pop music, a gutted Mass, theological shallowness, and "social justice" pabulum that was a proxy for far left politics.

Although Maranatha House and other Protestant groups also offered contemporary music in an informal setting, there was just something far more authentic and Christ-centered in those places than in the American Catholic Church's post-Vatican II attempts to be "relevant." What many of us young Catholics needed and desired were intelligent and winsome ambassadors for Christ who knew the intellectual basis for the Christian faith (and the Catholic faith in particular), respected and understood the solemnity and theological truths behind the liturgy, and who could explain the renewal movements in light of these. Although the Protestant churches I attended, for obvious reasons, could not provide all of that, they offered some of it. They were encouraging and enthusiastic about sharing their faith and were confident that they could defend it against the challenges of unbelief. The latter, which is called "apologetics," was, of course, not the staple of Protestant

Sunday services, but it had an important place in Evangelical Protestant bookstores, Sunday school classes, radio shows, and tape libraries. Because the Bible and its authenticity as God's inerrant Word was the touchstone belief that most Evangelical Protestants thought had to be defended against secular and liberal assaults, the Protestant churches also provided a presentation of Christ and his Church that was rooted in an ancient book, the Bible. This belief united non-Catholic Christians from a variety of Protestant denominations. For this reason, it would not be unusual for me to attend a service at Maranatha House and hear a teaching by a Methodist minister, while at the next two services hear sermons by Episcopalian and Baptist clergy.[4]

After leaving St. Viator Elementary School in 1974 following eighth grade, I attended Bishop Gorman High School. During my freshman year I began to drift away from Maranatha House and the Protestant churches I had attended. The reason was not theological. Maranatha House had become affiliated with a minister named Brother Abbott who told the group's members that the Lord was leading them to move to Salinas, California, to start a Christian commune. I found the whole idea creepy, and I just thought that Brother Abbott seemed a wee bit full of himself.[5]

I never ceased going to Mass with my family on Sunday, while attending a Protestant service or two during the week. However, once Maranatha House started to become weird, I stopped going to Protestant churches altogether until the end of my senior year in high school. Between the beginning of my sophomore year (1975) and February of my senior year (1978), I began to express doubts about my faith. I told some of my fellow Gorman students that I had become an agnostic, that I was not sure that God existed. I still attended Sunday Mass, in order to show respect for my parents and their beliefs. In retrospect, as I explain below, I am convinced that this "unbelief" was conjured up, that it was not sincerely held. For like most unreflective skeptics, I was not skeptical enough of my skepticism.

Whatever the case, my religion classes at Gorman were of no help in remedying these apparent doubts. Take, for example, my freshman religion class, which was taught by the varsity basket-

39

ball coach, who, to my knowledge, had no theological credentials whatsoever. This seemed to show that the school's administration lacked theological seriousness, for they would never have dreamed of hiring a theologian to coach the boy's basketball team. The basketball coach would often lead us in discussions about contemporary moral issues while offering no clear direction on how to acquire, or think through, the right answers. For instance, during one week of class he moderated a four on four debate between students about whether or not premarital sex was immoral. The Catholic Church, of course, has pronounced on this matter. But our teacher apparently did not think that he had an obligation to bring this to our attention, let alone offer to us the reasons why the Church held this position. Sadly, this was not an isolated occurrence of catechetical malfeasance. Serious discussions of theology were absent from all my religion classes. In one religion class we read and discussed Richard Bach's *Jonathan Livingston Seagull*, a 1970 New Age book about a seagull who learns about the true meaning of life congruent with his ability to soar higher.

Although the catechesis and religious instruction at Gorman was not as it should have been, in general my time there was a rewarding experience that has enriched my life and the lives of all my siblings. We are grateful for the sacrifices our parents made in order to send us to such a fine academic institution. As the only Catholic high school in Las Vegas (which is still the case), it provided (and still provides) to many of us a wonderful community of students and families.

Tangled Up in Blue

In the spring semester of my senior year (1977–78), I became very depressed. I should not have been. I was a member of the varsity basketball team that was about to travel to Reno for the AAA state championship (which we won, by the way!). I had lettered in two varsity sports, cross-country and basketball, with a third on the way later that spring in track. I had a great family and was doing well in school (though I was not a stellar student, largely because I was bored and lazy). Yet, I was unhappy. I believe that my unhappiness was the result of my skepticism about the truth of God and Christianity. I am also convinced, as I reflect on this period with the hindsight of three decades under my belt, that this skepticism was not sincere, that I actually conjured it up because I arrogantly thought that the burden of belief could be lifted by a mere act of my will. This is why, I believe, I never abandoned God or Christ. I thought I could avert the eyes of God by averting mine. It did not work.

During one afternoon in February 1978 I knelt down next to my bed and asked God to help me in my apparent unbelief. On my dresser behind me an FM radio blared a classic rock song. (I was, after all, a seventeen year old.) All of a sudden, moments after I had made my petition to God, the music on the radio seemed slowly to turn into white noise. As the white noise faded into the background I began to hear the voice of a disk jockey on the local Christian radio station. He was saying something about committing one's life to Christ. This was really spooky to me. So, I walked over to the radio to see what was going on. It was indeed tuned to the rock station, but the Christian station was overtaking the rock station, with white noise subtly fading in and out. I later learned from a friend that what happened to my FM radio is a naturally explicable phenomenon that sometimes occurs. But given the timing and content of my prayer, the radio stations involved, and the DJ's message, I have never ceased to think of that incident as a gentle tap on my shoulder from the Lord who knew that I had never really stopped believing in him.

I wasn't sure what to do. So the next day I called the man who had taken me to Maranatha House when I was in seventh grade. He suggested I talk with an Evangelical Protestant public school teacher who was living nearby.

I visited with Russell. We talked for about thirty minutes. He then offered to pray with me so that I could ask the Lord back into my life.[6] After we prayed, Russell hooked me up with a weekly Bible study, in which I participated for the next three years. I soon became a regular Sunday attendee of Neighborhood Foursquare Church in Henderson, Nevada, as well as its youth offshoot called Fish City, that met for song, teaching, fellowship, and prayer on Monday nights.

In late February 1979 I broke my ankle, and tore all of its liga-ments, while playing a pick-up basketball game with a bunch of high school friends. Because I could not play basketball or jog for three months, I was holed up at my parents' home most of the time when I was not in school. I filled the days by reading books and teaching myself how to play guitar. These months of solitude opened up a whole new side of me that I did not know existed. I devoured far more tomes in philosophy, theology, and history than I had previously thought I was capable of consuming, let alone understanding. I also began writing poems, some of which served as lyrics for songs I would compose with my guitar.

My Aunt Doris, who was living with us at the time (with two of her sons), would often sit up at night with me and patiently listen to me recite my many works. She was always encouraging and seemed to like my poems very much. Aunt Doris was a sweet lady with an enormous capacity for generosity and empathy. This was all the more miraculous given that she had undergone enormous suffering in a tumultuous existence that included decades of a dysfunctional family life. The poetry writing continued into my late twenties. When I was dating my future wife, Frankie, I would often write poems to her.

In fall 1979 I attended several lectures by Walter R. Martin (1929–89), a popular Christian apologist, original host of the *Bible Answer Man* radio program, and well-known as the author of *The Kingdom of the Cults*. He really impressed me. He had a deep knowledge of scripture, a kind of street-wise though so-phisticated New York City demeanor (which reminded me of my parents and their siblings), and he was quick on his feet. He would end his lectures with about forty-five minutes of questions from the audience.

Years later I would hear a wonderful story about Walter Mar-tin from Fr. Mitch Pacwa, SJ, a former theology professor at the University of Dallas who hosts *EWTN Live*, a weekly talk show broadcast on the Catholic cable television network, EWTN (Eternal Word Television Network). I met Martin only twice, but Father Pacwa had known him quite well. They had debated each other on several occasions, which resulted in a long-term friendship that included Fr. Pacwa contributing to and serving on the editorial board of *Christian Research Journal*,[7] the publication of the Christian Research Institute, whose founding president was Walter Martin. (Interestingly enough, I have served on the same editorial board since 1987, and continue to serve, at the request of the editor Elliot Miller, even though I have become Catholic.) According to Fr. Pacwa, he had been invited by Martin to attend his ordination to become a Southern Baptist minister. The minister officiating the ceremony asked all the ordained ministers present to come forward and participate with him in laying hands on Martin. Fr. Pacwa, a Catholic priest, remained in his seat, not wanting to cause offense to his Protestant brethren by walking up to the front of the sanctuary while wearing his Roman collar. Martin, who had his head bowed, lifted it up and looked directly at Fr. Pacwa and said in his deep, booming voice, "He said 'all ordained ministers.'" Fr. Pacwa then left his seat, proceeded to the front, and placed his hands on Martin while the words of ordination were uttered by the Protestant celebrant. After telling me this story, Fr. Pacwa chuckled, "You can now tell your Protestant friends that a Catholic priest helped ordain Walter Martin."

Now back to 1979. Because I had listened to some of Walter Martin's tapes years earlier when I was attending Maranatha House, it was a delight to hear and see him in person for the first time. Martin ended his last night of lectures with this challenge to the audience: "You should pray and ask the Lord if he is calling you to a ministry in apologetics." I took Martin's advice and prayed. The next afternoon, after returning from school, two Mormon missionaries were at my door. Although my prayers seemed to be answered, I did not know exactly what to do. So, I asked the missionaries to come back in a couple of weeks. In the interim, I called the church at which Martin had lectured and asked for some help. The church put me in contact with a young Las Vegas High School science teacher named Danny Green, who had helped bring Martin to Las Vegas. Danny is a terrific lay apologist who, over the years, put me in contact with the works of many Christian writers including Francis A. Schaeffer, C. Everett Koop, Norman L. Geisler, Arnold G. Fruchtenbaum, and John Warwick Montgomery. (I had heard Montgomery's tapes years earlier, as I had heard Martin's. But reading Montgomery was a real treat. He was an Evangelical Protestant with impressive academic credentials who really knew how to turn a phrase. A couple of years later I would find myself under his tutelage at Simon Greenleaf University.) Danny also provided me with a variety of resources about Mormonism (the Church of Jesus Christ of Latter-day Saints [LDS])—including the works of former Mormons Jerald and Sandra Tanner—so that I could effectively dialogue with the missionaries when they returned to my home.

This interest in Mormon theology never waned. After earning my PhD at Fordham University in 1989, I published two books and several academic articles on LDS beliefs.[8] What was especially gratifying about my second book on Mormonism was that it was taken seriously by LDS scholars, two of which wrote book jacket endorsements: Brigham Young University Professor Daniel Peterson and LDS philosopher Blake Ostler. I say all this because one of the lessons that I learned from the examples set by both my parents and Dan Green is that when you disagree with another person you must not forget that that individual is still entitled to both your respect as well as your Christian charity. This is why I have always tried my best to offer my criticisms of LDS thought in measured tones rather than with inflammatory rhetoric, which, sadly, is not atypical in some quarters of Christianity.[9]

Danny Green has since become a strong Calvinist, having come under the influence of the writings of Michael Scott Horton and R. C. Sproul. This, however, does not surprise me. For my experience has been that most very intelligent Christians who had come to a deeper walk with Christ in independent Evangelical and/or non-liturgical churches often gravitate toward a theological and/or ecclesiastical tradition that has strong historical roots, such as Calvinism, Lutheranism, Catholicism, or Eastern Orthodoxy.

Danny and I are still very close friends, even though I know he is not entirely comfortable with my return to Catholicism. Nevertheless, he has been for Frankie and me such a wonderful exemplar of Christ's love and compassion. In 2005 he lost both his wife and his mother, and showed enormous courage and fortitude through it all. His wife, Debbie, died unexpectedly in February 2005 due to complications arising from her rheumatoid arthritis. Only seven months later, in September, Danny was informed by relatives that his mother had drowned in a flood that resulted from the devastation of Hurricane Katrina in Danny's native New Orleans. The care and love that Danny showed to his wife during her many years of suffering, as well as the strength he exhibited after his mother's passing, were for many of us such a powerful witness of his devotion to Christ and the Gospel.

I would be remiss if I did not point out that virtually every Evangelical Protestant I knew during this time was a former Catholic. And I know that my story is not an isolated one in that regard, for I have met hundreds of former Catholics around the United States who are now (or were, until they returned to the Church) committed Evangelical Protestants trying to follow Christ the best they can. In light of this, the American Catholic Church has to ask itself a serious and painful question: is there anything that we did that helped facilitate the departure of these talented and devoted people from our communion?

3

Summa Apologia

> Just as it is greater to illuminate than merely to shine, so too it is greater to give to others what one has contemplated than merely to contemplate.
>
> St. Thomas Aquinas, from *Summa Theologiae*[1]

graduated from the University of Nevada, Las Vegas (UNLV) in 1983. I had switched my major two years earlier from journalism to philosophy as I became interested in studying theology more formally in graduate school. Advice from mentors, my undergraduate studies, and my wide reading in theology had convinced me that even if I were to study apologetics more formally in graduate school, philosophy was the discipline in which I should earn my doctorate.

It seemed to me that philosophy has a unique and important role to play in our understanding of the nature of knowledge and its relationship to Christian faith and its rationality. "Philosophy," according to my friend J. P. Moreland, "operates as a second-order discipline that investigates other disciplines."[2] What he means is that the primary task of the philosopher is to critically examine the logical, metaphysical, and empirical foundations of particular disciplines and beliefs. For example, an attorney, a specialist in the first-order discipline of law, is the person one ought to consult concerning one's rights pertaining to the area of law in question, for example, property law, criminal law, tort law, etc. On the other hand, a *philosopher of law* tries to answer such questions as "What is a right?" "What is the nature of rights?" or "Is there a natural law that transcends culture?" The theologian is the person best suited to answer questions concerning religious history, biblical theology, or dogmatics. On the other hand, the *philosopher of religion* seeks to find answers to questions such as, "Is it rational to believe in God?" "Are God's attributes logically coherent?" "Are miracles possible?"

My mother tells me that she can recall an early interest in philosophy on my part, though at the time it seemed to her that I was "just being a smart aleck." At age nine I offered to my mother a typical nine-year-old's reason as to why I should be allowed to participate with the older children in what we in southern Nevada called "dirt clod fights," a southwestern desert version of "snow ball fights." When my mother banned me from this activity, I pleaded, "But all the other kids are playing." She responded with that familiar parental quip: "But what if all the kids were jumping off the roof?" I offered this reply, a type of *reductio ad absurdum* (though I surely did not know the nomenclature at the time), "But what if *you* told me to jump off the roof, like you're telling me I can't play with the other kids in the dirt clod fights?" Corporal punishment followed.

Simon Greenleaf

In January 1983, the apologist Walter Martin was back for a visit in Las Vegas. I was delighted to share a dinner with him. I discussed with Martin my interests in philosophy and apologetics. He then told me about a new Christian school in southern California called the Simon Greenleaf School of Law (later called Simon Greenleaf University). It was named after the famous Harvard Law School expert on evidence who authored *The Testimony of the Evangelists* (1874), a book that applied to the Christian Gospels the legal rules of evidence in order to show their authenticity. Martin was on a faculty that included the school's founding dean, John Warwick Montgomery, as well as Harold Lindsell (one of the founders of Fuller Theological Seminary and author of the controversial 1978 book *The Battle for the Bible*), Charles Manske (founding president of Concordia University, Irvine), and Lutheran theologian Rodney Rosenblatt. Although Simon Greenleaf was primarily a law school that offered the standard JD degree, it also had an MA program in Christian apologetics. I applied for the MA program and was offered admission.

Montgomery had left his tenured faculty position at Trinity Evangelical Divinity School (TEDS) in the mid-1970s and eventually wound up in southern California, where in 1980 he founded Simon Greenleaf. Ironically, in 1997 Greenleaf merged with Trinity International University (of which TEDS is a part), eight years after Montgomery stepped down as Simon Greenleaf's dean. That's the same Trinity that hired me to be a faculty member in 1997 at its California campus, the former Simon Greenleaf.

Montgomery was not your typical American Evangelical. He drove a 1940s-style luxury automobile that was the sort of vehicle one would imagine had transported General Franco across Madrid. A Lutheran with a strong background in historical theology, he was a wine connoisseur with an interest in the culinary arts of a variety of European nations, especially France. With eight earned degrees at the time (including a PhD from the University of Chicago, a ThD from the University of Strausborg, and a law degree), Montgomery had a certain literary flair that was absent from most of the subdued Midwestern Reformed types that dominated the Evangelical world. He had interests in philosophy of science, historiography, the occult, church history, biblical theology, jurisprudence, and literature (especially the works of C. S. Lewis, G. K. Chesterton, J. R. R. Tolkein, and George McDonald). And in all these areas he had published well-written essays, articles, and books that attracted many young Evangelicals, such as myself, to the life of the mind. His public debates are legendary. For example, in 1967 he debated Thomas J. J. Altizer, a leader in the famous "Death of God" movement in the 1960s. At the University of Chicago in early 1967, Montgomery simply decimated Altizer in one of the most amazing intellectual smack-downs ever recorded. Politically, he was a kind of American version of a European Christian Democrat. He was conservative on social issues, such as abortion and homosexuality, but fairly liberal on matters like health care and religious disestablishment. So, it was not unusal for Montgomery to offer trenchant and thoughtful critiques of both the Religious Right and the Religious Left. He also had a penchant for colorful clothing. It would not be unusual to see Montgomery delivering a paper at an academic conference wearing a felt plaid green dinner jacket and orange pants.

Given Simon Greenleaf's newness (it was founded in 1980) and lack of regional accreditation, I should have probably tried to go to a more established institution for my master's degree. But I was young and did not know any better. Nevertheless, I do not regret my decision to attend and earn a degree from Simon Greenleaf. For I did indeed receive a solid education under the tutelage of Lutheran theologians Manske and Montgomery, as well as church history professor Michael Smythe and other professors in New Testament Greek and biblical criticism and authenticity. Dr. Montgomery taught an amazing history of apologetics course that took us from the New Testament Church through the Patristic Period and the Middle Ages to the Reformation, the Enlightenment, and contemporary times. In both Montgomery's and Smythe's classes I was, for the first time in my life, able to formally study the Reformation and its relationship to prior and subsequent Christian thought. Although I was a committed Protestant years before I arrived at Greenleaf, my experience and study there helped me to better appreciate the historical and theological roots of that commitment.

Because of Greenleaf's rigorous thesis requirement for its MA students, I had to write an extended and detailed work of scholarship that exceeded anything I had ever written before. I also had to publicly defend it. Not only did that thesis work help prepare me for the research and writing that was required for my PhD dissertation at Fordham University several years later, I wound up publishing a revised version of the thesis as a book with Bethany House Publishers, *Baha'i* (1985). Looking back I confess I was far too young (24 years old) to publish a book that offered a critical assessment of a world religion. I had not read as deeply or carefully as I should have—nor did I possess the charitable spirit a Christian ought to have when writing a polemical tome about another faith.[3]

Because Greenleaf was broadly ecumenical, its students and faculty consisted of Evangelical Protestants from a wide variety of traditions and backgrounds. I had arrived at the school with a pretty narrow Protestant experience, knowing only free church, dispensationalist, and charismatic types. Thus, I was surprised to find high church, middle church, and non-dispensationalist Protestants among my professors and peers. Although many of the students were free church Evangelical types like me, some were not. Even among the free church Evangelicals, many were exploring Christian literature outside their ecclesiastical patrimony. It was at Greenleaf that I was introduced to the writings of G. K. Chesterton. I was quickly mesmerized by his wit, wisdom, and insight. Chesterton, I later found out, was a Catholic convert from Anglicanism. But, unlike some Protestant Evangelicals who have a visceral reaction to anything Catholic, I thought nothing of Chesterton's Catholicism. After all, given my already budding commitment to the philosophical work of the great doctor of the Catholic Church, Thomas Aquinas (from having imbibed the writings of Norman Geisler, an Evangelical Protestant Thomist), I had no doubt that a Protestant could gain real theological insights from Catholic authors.

Fordham and Grandma Guido

During my time at Greenleaf I had become even more convinced that I needed to earn a PhD in philosophy if I wanted to become a better Christian apologist. I applied to several graduate programs. My mother suggested that I apply to Fordham University, a Jesuit institution in New York City. So, I requested a catalog and application. When the materials arrived in the mail, I was impressed with the philosophy department's emphasis on the history of philosophy as well as the diversity of faculty interests in specific areas of study (e.g., ethics, philosophy of religion, philosophy of law, metaphysics). I was accepted into Fordham's PhD program in philosophy and subsequently received a full fellowship.

In late August 1984 I moved to New York City to attend Fordham, located in the Bronx. I lived in the Cypress Hills section of Brooklyn with my maternal grandmother, Frances Guido, an Italian-American and devout Catholic whose parents emigrated from Sicily at the turn of the century. Born in 1913 (d. 2002), my grandmother was an amazing woman. She lost her husband (my grandfather) to stomach cancer in 1952. Widowed at the age of thirty-eight, she worked as a seamstress and provided each of her four children with twelve years of Catholic-school education.

I once asked my grandmother why she never remarried. Her answer initially seemed stunning to me, though, given her beliefs and convictions, it made perfect sense. She said, "How can I bring a strange man into a home with two young daughters?" What an amazing (and politically incorrect) answer. Her first thought was not of herself and what she should have wanted. It was about what advanced the common good, and in this case, the good of her family and her young children. What my grandmother's understanding manifested was the incarnational faith of which Jesus spoke when he told his disciples that "whoever would save his life will lose it; and whoever loses his life for my sake and the gospel's will save it" (Mark 8:35).

Living with my grandmother was an incredible experience. She exhibited the love of Christ in everything she did, even when she was angry with me for having a messy bedroom. One time, for instance, while cleaning the house, she said, "You know, Lincoln freed the slaves." I answered, "But not the Italian ones," at which she laughed and said that just because I was funny didn't mean she wasn't mad.

My grandmother's charity seemed boundless. For example, in 1974, while my younger brother James and I were spending a month of that summer at my grandmother's apartment in Brooklyn, our mother called and told us that one of my eighth grade classmates was in a hospital in Manhattan receiving treatment for a cancerous tumor that was found in his upper leg. We had tickets to a New York Mets game for the next day. My grandmother suggested that after the game we go visit him in the hospital and bring a baseball to him as a gift. So, we did. During the visit my grandmother met his mother, Louise. They quickly became friends. Within weeks my grandmother had convinced Louise that she should stay at my grandmother's apartment whenever her son had to be in New York for treatments. For the next several years, my grandmother opened her home and her heart to my classmate's family as they suffered through his cancer and his death, as well as those of his father and two sisters. My grandmother, who had been widowed in 1952, knew the heartache of an untimely death and the trials that accompany it. Her compassion, her willingness to "suffer with" others, truly revealed the spirit of Christ that worked in her heart. I must confess, however, that it is only in retrospect that I have come to appreciate how her example left an indelible mark on so many of those with whom she came in contact, including me, her eldest grandchild.

She went to Mass every morning and was involved with many works of mercy at her parish. Whenever there was sickness, death, or heartache among her friends or family, she was there, prepared to cook, clean, say the rosary, or just listen. We were always hosting dinners or lunches with family and friends, or else traveling via subway, bus, or automobile to visit aunts, uncles, cousins, or other relatives whose genetic connection to me I'm still not sure about.

My grandmother kept her mind alert by reading, doing crossword puzzles every night, and arguing with me about politics. She was a Franklin Roosevelt Democrat, and I was a Ronald Reagan Republican. Our bantering was always friendly, but mischievous. Whenever there was a negative story in the newspaper or on television, no matter how distant or obscure, for which she could blame President Reagan, she made sure I knew about it. On the November night that President Reagan was reelected in 1984, with a 49-state landslide, my grandma graciously conceded defeat and congratulated Reagan for his triumph, though she did go on to say that Reagan was a better actor than a president and he wasn't even a good actor. I respectfully did not take the bait.

Grandma Guido was pleased that I was attending a Catholic university. She obviously knew that I was Protestant, but she seemed confident that some of my professor-priests would help steer me back to the Church. Although my time at Fordham did not result in my return to the Catholic Church, it is fair to say that because I studied under some of the finest philosophical minds American Catholicism had to offer, I acquired a deeper appreciation of the philosophical underpinnings of Catholic theology and its relationship to the histories of philosophy and Christian thought. This understanding helped form and shape my views on God's nature, the human person, and the natural moral law. But none of these views seemed to me at the time inconsistent with Protestant theology, as the works of some Thomistic and Thomas-friendly Evangelical Protestant thinkers clearly showed.

My professors included the great Thomist philosopher W. Norris Clarke, SJ, from whom I took courses on both Thomas Aquinas and metaphysics. There were no assigned textbooks for those classes except Fr. Clarke's mimeographed notes, of which I still have copies and occasionally consult. It was up to the students to acquire the writings of the works we covered, which meant that I spent an enormous amount of time combing Fordham's library shelves. Fr. Clarke was an amazing teacher. He not only knew his subject well and how to communicate it effectively, but he also exuded a sense of Christian joy and contentment that set a wonderful example for young aspiring Christian philosophers.

I also studied under Gerald McCool, SJ, from whom I took Medieval Humanism. He was part philosopher and part stand-up comic, a true scholar with a spontaneous and effective wit. For instance, one day in class when we were studying Pseudo-Dionysius he went on a long verbal excursion into neo-Platonism's denigration of the physical world (including the body) and began singing an on-the-spot parody version of the song, "Just a Gigolo." He crooned the line, "I ain't got nobody," pronouncing the phrase "no body."

My other professors included Dominic Balestsra, Quentin Lauer, SJ, Merold Westphal, and my dissertation advisor, Robert Roth, SJ. Fr. Roth was about two years away from retirement when I asked him to be my advisor. He consented, but under the conditions that

I complete it in eighteen months and that it not exceed 300 pages. A specialist in British Empiricism and American Pragmatism, Fr. Roth was a perfect mentor for the topic of my dissertation, *David Hume's Argument Against Miracles: Contemporary Attempts to Rehabilitate It and a Response* (1988). Not only did his critical comments help make the work better than it otherwise would have been, but he also gave me some good advice that I have passed on to a number of my own doctoral students over the years. He said, "Remember, Frank, your dissertation is the beginning, not the end. So, don't think that it's your magnum opus. You don't know enough to write anything like that."

During my second year in New York City I had the opportunity to meet Edith Schaeffer, the widow of the Presbyterian theologian Francis A. Schaeffer (1912–84), whose published works were influential in my decision to pursue graduate work in philosophy. Mrs. Schaeffer was in New York for a book-signing event at the massive Christian Book Distributors retail outlet in Midtown Manhattan. When I arrived there in the mid-afternoon, the crowds had dissipated and Mrs. Schaeffer was sitting alone at a table. I introduced myself to her and told her about her late husband's influence on me. She seemed sincerely interested in my story. She then kindly asked if I wanted her to sign one of her books. I said "yes," and handed her a copy of *Common Sense Christian Living*. She then opened up the book to the first blank page and proceeded to draw a sketch of the Swiss Alps, with birds flying between the mountains and a small flower at the base. (For years, she and her husband lived in Switzerland where they founded the ministry L'Abri). She then wrote in large letters:

> *April 29, 1986*
> *To Francis with love, Edith Schaeffer. I've*
> *written many notes to another Francis—I do pray*
> *your life may be as significant in History.*

It was only when I reread Mrs. Schaeffer's inscription while writing this book that I realized that the day of her written prayer for me is the same day that in 2007 I was publicly received back into the Catholic Church, April 29. This is one of those "coincidences" that really spooks me, but in a good way.

I lived with my grandmother for three years between August 1984 and May 1987, except during Christmas vacations and the summers. During those summers I worked for my father in Las Vegas at The Dunes Hotel & Casino, either monitoring the gambling activity of customers who came in from California bus junkets or working on a variety of different projects in internal auditing where my father served as the director. However, I did return to Vegas for one Fordham spring break, a fateful one in March 1985. While in Vegas I became reacquainted with Frankie Dickerson (my future wife), the sister of my friend Lexi Weigand. Lexi's husband Mark was instrumental in helping to lead Frankie to Christ at Calvary Chapel Costa Mesa on July 11, 1982. (Coincidentally or providentially, July 11 is our wedding anniversary as well as the feast day of St. Benedict, the namesake of the Pope under whose papacy Frankie joined, and I returned to, the Catholic Church.) Although I had known Frankie for several years, I had never had any romantic interest in her, until this spring break. For some strange reason, I had not noticed her. And she had not noticed me either, largely because, as she never tires telling me, she had seen me as a pocket protector–wearing nice but nerdy guy with unkempt hair who was wardrobe challenged. Apparently, my brief time in New York had changed that. I had learned how to dress and present myself more attractively.

When I returned to Las Vegas in summer 1985, Frankie and I began spending a lot of time together. We both attended Vineyard Christian Fellowship, where I taught an adult Sunday School class on Christian apologetics. I began to really fall for Frankie, and it seemed that she was feeling the same about me. But she was a little nervous. So, before I returned to New York at summer's end, she told me that she liked me but that we should be "just friends." Although I was devastated, the blow was cushioned by what I had read in Dr. James Dobson's 1983 book, *Love Must Be Tough*, which Frankie had recommended to me weeks earlier. She apparently knew that Dr. Dobson could offer me insights that would help me understand her. He suggested that in situations such as mine, the worst thing that a man could do is grovel and plead for a woman's affection like some pouting puppy dog. Taking Dr. Dobson's advice, I did not contact Frankie for six weeks after my return to New York. It was initially difficult, but as the days wore on the pain of rejection dissipated. In fact, after those six weeks I began to share with my "friend" Frankie about women that I had met at Fordham, including an attractive Puerto Rican doctoral student in sociology with whom I went to church several Sundays in a row. A few days after I had shared this with Frankie, she sent me a hand-written letter in which she explained that her affection for me was more than that of mere friendship. By August 1986 we were engaged. We were married the next July.

New Friends and Influences

During my second year at Fordham I met Michael Bauman, a professor at Northeastern Bible College in New Jersey. Mike was a 1983 Fordham PhD graduate in theology and literature. An Evangelical Protestant, he was also the book review editor of the *Journal of the Evangelical Theological Society* (JETS), the academic periodical of the Evangelical Theological Society, which I had joined in 1984. Several weeks before I met Mike I mailed a note to him at his Northeastern Bible College office asking if there were any books in my areas of interest I could review for JETS. Instead of replying via the post office, Mike placed a note under the door of the office I shared with several other graduate assistants in the philosophy department. It turned out that Mike had an office at Fordham two doors down from mine. He was teaching a course on Reformation theology while the professor who ordinarily taught the course was on leave. We met face to face days later. It was the beginning of an enduring friendship.

In 1988 Mike moved to Hillsdale College, in Michigan, where he is still on the faculty. In addition to his friendship and counsel, Mike's clarity of mind and thought, as well as his writing style and penetrating intellect, have been important resources in my own professional and spiritual development. Even though Mike remains a committed Protestant, and behind the scenes asked me some serious though fair questions about my return to the Catholic Church soon after it took place, our friendship and shared devotion to the Christian faith continues without hiccup or pause. We have coedited two books,[4] and we have both served since 1996 on the faculty of Summit Ministries (Manitou Springs, Colorado), which offers seven two-week summer conferences on the Christian worldview for sixteen- to twenty-year-old Christians.

During my time at Fordham and while working on my doctoral dissertation I began to make connections with other Evangelical scholars. Among those with whom I became close friends are William Lane Craig, Gary R. Habermas, Norman L. Geisler, and J. P. Moreland. Over the years we have endorsed and contributed to each others' books and have participated together in many conferences, courses, and panel discussions.

Although my Thomistic leanings were reinforced and solidified as a result of my Fordham experience, during that time I also began to read more widely in Christian philosophy and apologetics in other Christian traditions. I explored the works of supporters of what is called "Reformed epistemology," including Ronald H. Nash (with whom I would later become friends), Alvin Plantinga, and Nicholas Wolterstorff. The term "epistemology" literally means "theory of knowledge" and it refers to a subdiscipline in philosophy that investigates questions having to do with how and why our minds acquire knowledge and what counts as knowledge. (For example: if you reject the conclusions of a fortune-teller because you think you have good reason to believe that fortune-telling does not result in reliable knowledge, then you are making an epistemological judgment.) The "Reformed" part of "Reformed epistemology" refers to the theological tradition that has its roots in the work of the Protestant Reformer John Calvin. Philosophers who defend Reformed epistemology believe they are offering an account of knowledge supported by Calvin's teachings and by implication the teachings of scripture, since Calvin embraced the principle of *sola scriptura* (or "scripture alone").

Reformed epistemologists challenge what is called the "evidential objection to belief in God," the view that in order for belief in God to be rational one needs sufficient evidence in order to hold it. To qualify as sufficient, evidence must be the result of the deliverances of the senses and/or logical reasoning, the foundation of all knowledge. According to Reformed epistemologists, the evidentialist objection to belief in God fails on several counts: (1) It is self-refuting, since the view that a belief requires sufficient evidence in order to be rational is itself a belief that the evidentialist holds without evidence, for it functions as a first principle. (2) There are many beliefs that are perfectly rational to hold that we do not infer from evidence—for example, "It is wrong to torture children for fun," "The universe did not come into being five minutes ago with all the appearances, memories, and experiences as if it were billions of years old," "The Grand Canyon is majestic." (3) It seems to most people that belief in God makes perfect sense given their own personal histories, sense of wonder, religious experience, understanding of their own moral and spiritual shortcomings, and so on. That is, belief in God is immediately produced, not as the result of an inference from evidence (as one would infer an "accident" from a smelly baby), but much like our belief that there are other minds. We don't believe in other minds because we gather evidence and infer that belief. Rather, belief in other minds is part of the infrastructure of our lives that is perfectly rational to believe without "evidence."

The Reformed epistemologists are not saying that theism, and Christianity in particular, cannot be supported by evidence. Rather, they are arguing that belief in God, like many of our other beliefs, need not be based on evidence in order to be rationally held.

My reading of the Reformed epistemologists was a real eye-opening experience, since my only encounter with this tradition in Christian philosophy was through the works of John Warwick Montgomery, who, though a wonderful scholar and teacher, did not offer to his students a sympathetic reading of this school of thought. Montgomery, unfortunately, seemed smitten by a particular way of doing Christian apologetics that bought into a view of rationality that the Reformed thinkers, rightfully, I believe, saw as not only philosophically flawed but deleterious to Christian faith. (Montgomery is a self-described "evidentialist.") While I have never embraced Reformed epistemology whole hog, I have learned much from these Reformed thinkers about why it is important to critically assess philosophical views that are inconsistent with the foundations of Christian belief that some Christians may be tempted to assimilate, without realizing how these views (though in some cases seemingly benign) may have the effect of undermining Christian belief. For this reason, serious Catholic philosophers, including Thomists, have much to contribute to the goal of Reformed epistemology, namely, to dismantle a narrow view of "rationality" that not only squeezes out Christian belief, but also has deep philosophical flaws.

Due to the combined influences of Montgomery, Reformed theology, and my Fordham professors, as the end of the 1980s approached, I had become convinced that the Catholic creeds (the Apostles' Creed, the Nicene Creed, and the Athanasian Creed), the deliverances of the first six ecumenical councils,[5] as well as the canons of the Synod of Orange (AD 529), were authoritative renderings of Christian doctrine. I was also convinced that I believed this because these ecclesiastical pronouncements were derived exclusively from biblical exegesis and nothing more. Since I had studied the works of quasi-Christian groups (such as the Mormon church) that denied the veracity of the Catholic creeds because they were deemed "extra biblical" I was driven to a deep respect and appreciation for the formulation and promulgation of the Catholic creeds, which are embraced as normative by most Protestants.[6] Of course, I read these creeds and councils with "Protestant eyes," and thus I missed much of their carefully crafted language, what they assumed and asserted ecclesiastically, and when they occurred historically, all of which would play a part in establishing a first premise in an internal conversation that led to my return to the Catholic Church nearly two decades later.

4

No Direction Home

Whoever afflict us, whatever surround
Life is a voyage that's homeward-bound!

Herman Melville, from *White-Jacket
or the World in a Man-of-War* (1892)[1]

In 1989, two years after Frankie and I married, I began a faculty
appointment in the Philosophy Department at the University of
Nevada, Las Vegas (UNLV). I remained there until 1996, when I
was offered and accepted a position at Whittier College in southern
California. During most of our days in Las Vegas we were members of Christian Life Community, an independent Evangelical
charismatic church on whose elder board I served.

Probably my most memorable encounter at UNLV occurred in
1996 and involved another Roman Catholic intellectual. The conservative writer and thinker, William F. Buckley Jr., was at UNLV
for a debate with John Kenneth Galbraith, the economist with
whom he debated numerous times. Mr. Buckley was the founder of
the magazine *National Review*, to which I had subscribed during
my years at Fordham. Three of my books have received positive
reviews in *National Review*,[2] and I have contributed articles to
National Review Online over the years.

Frankie and I snuck into the room where Mr. Buckley was resting before the UNLV debate. We were amazed to find him alone. We introduced ourselves to him. He immediately began asking me questions about my academic work. I told him that I had published a book (*Politically Correct Death: Answering the Arguments for Abortion Rights*) that had been one of the two featured volumes by the Conservative Book Club during a month in 1994. I proudly told him that the other selected book for that month was one of his. He then said, in his distinct style, "That's similar to when my son Chris and I both had books on the *New York Times* bestsellers list at the same time." I thought to myself, "No, it isn't." He, of course, was just trying to be kind. And I very much appreciated that. He then turned his attention to my wife and asked her a variety of questions about living in Las Vegas with a philosopher.

Frankie then asked Mr. Buckley if he would allow one of my students to take a picture of the three of us. He agreed. Right before the photo was taken, I was standing next to Mr. Buckley and my wife was to his left. He then gently grasped her shoulders from behind, escorted her between us, turned to me and said, "A rose between two thorns."

A university official then arrived to take Mr. Buckley to the theater at which the debate was to take place. I didn't get a chance to tell him that his work—especially the 1959 book *Up From Liberalism*—strongly influenced my developing political views while I was in college and graduate school. While reading the book as an undergraduate I found myself agreeing with its arguments before I knew that the author was a "conservative." In fact, when I told one of my professors that I was reading *Up From Liberalism* and thought it was terrific and compelling, my professor said, "But Buckley is a conservative. You can't possibly agree with him." I then said, "I guess I am a conservative."

Southern California

We left Las Vegas in the summer of 1996 and I began my faculty appointment at Whittier College. Within six months of my first year at Whittier, I received an offer from the provost of Trinity

International University (Deerfield, Illinois), Nigel Cameron. He asked if I would consider joining the faculty of the school's new California campus, where I would teach in its new MA program in faith and culture in its new graduate school. With a higher salary and rank, a lighter teaching load, and no need to move out of our new home in Anaheim Hills (which was located closer to Trinity's California campus than to Whittier), it didn't take me long to formally accept the offer.

TIU is a Evangelical Protestant school that is affiliated with the Evangelical Free Church of America. Because I also had faculty status in the university's seminary, Trinity Evangelical Divinity School, I thought it was appropriate that I become an ordained minister. And since I had been for over fifteen years a frequent guest speaker in a variety of churches and for many Christian ministries, ordination seemed to make sense. So I became an ordained minister of the United Evangelical Churches. (I later resigned my ordination, days before I returned to full communion with the Catholic Church.)

In fall 1997, Trinity's comptroller, John Hughes (who has since, like me, returned to the Catholic Church of his baptism), invited Frankie and me to attend church with him and his family at St. Luke's Reformed Episcopal Church, in Santa Ana. I had told John that we were having a difficult time finding a good Evangelical church in which we would fit. When Frankie and I walked in the building, she turned to me and said, "This almost seems Catholic." And sure enough, St. Luke's followed the liturgy found in the Book of Common Prayer, which is similar to the Catholic liturgy. It was my first experience in a Protestant church with a seriously liturgical service.

Because we liked St. Luke's and its Sunday service, I became interested in studying more deeply the history of Episcopalianism and its beliefs. When one of my Trinity Law School colleagues, Myron Steeves, caught wind of this, he invited Frankie and me to join him and his wife, Patty, one Sunday at St. James Episcopal Church, in Newport Beach. Unlike St. Luke's and its denomination, the Reformed Episcopal Church, St. James was in full communion with the Archbishop of Canterbury. We attended intermittently for several weeks but soon found ourselves regular members. Until our move to Princeton in July 2002, St. James was our home church. The church's rector for most of our time there was the Reverend (now Bishop) David Anderson. He was instrumental in helping found the American Anglican Council (AAC), a group of clergy, churches, and laymen within American Episcopalianism that were fighting the church's drift away from orthodoxy and into theological liberalism. St. James in some ways was ground zero in the fight for the soul of American Anglicanism.

It was during this time that my wife, Frankie, asked me: why aren't we Catholic? For her, the Anglican liturgy and solemnity of worship seemed nearly indistinguishable from the Masses we attended with my family. Frankie was also drawn by, and became quite interested in, the spirit of Christ she observed in Pope John Paul II. I explained to her that although I respected the Pope and considered his work as essential to displacing the materialism and unbelief that had overtaken Europe (and seemed to be gaining a foothold in America), I had too many theological problems with Catholicism. My reasons included the Church's views on justification, the Eucharist, and the papacy. She said, "I guess you're the theologian in the family. So I'll trust your judgment." (O ye of too much faith!)

Because I had negotiated an early sabbatical leave with Trinity, I spent the 2000–2001 school year at the Washington University School of Law in St. Louis, where I earned a Master of Juridical Studies degree. I did this because I had always had an interest in law (including jurisprudence and church-state issues), which I acquired during my time as a student at Simon Greenleaf. But I had neither the time nor the money nor the career aspirations to spend three years earning the professional degree in law, the Juris Doctorate (JD). I did not want to practice law, but I did want to study it. The degree I did earn allowed me to do this in a formal setting at a premier university while producing a work of scholarship (the dissertation) that I would publish as a book and several law review articles.

After law school, I returned to Trinity and taught there for one year, until another opportunity came my way. I had applied for, and was offered, a visiting full-time faculty appointment at Princeton

University for the 2002–03 school year. Among the other visiting fellows at Princeton that year was Hadley Arkes, a legal philosopher from Amherst College. I had known Hadley for eight years, having met him in 1994 at Fordham University when he gave the keynote address at the annual meeting of the University Faculty for Life. Hadley's works on jurisprudence and politics, as well as his writing style, which is an unusual though magnetic combination of philosophical rigor, literary flair, and mischievous genius, shaped the trajectory of my own professional aspirations. It helped expand my interests, which had been mostly in philosophy of religion and applied ethics, to include law and politics.

One night soon after we arrived at Princeton, Hadley called me at home to discuss several matters. In the midst of our conversation he asked, "Why are you a Protestant rather than a Catholic? Didn't you grow up Catholic?" This line of questioning took me by surprise, since Hadley was Jewish and we had never discussed our faiths with one another, even though we had known each other for nearly a decade. I gave him the standard Protestant theological responses, ones that I firmly believed were adequate for the task at hand. He paused for a moment and said, "That's all? That's it? You were brought up Catholic. Your parents are Catholic. I don't see why you don't return to the Church." I replied, "Hadley, you're Jewish, and for you, once you get past the 'Jesus thing' it's just down hill from there. But for Protestants and Catholics these are big issues." He chuckled and then asked if I would be interested in engaging in a private discussion with him and Robert P. George (a Catholic and Princeton professor) on the differences between Protestantism and Catholicism. Although that discussion never took place, Hadley's inquiry about my transition from Catholicism to Protestantism was the first time someone outside my immediate family had asked me such a question. As I tell in the next chapter, it would not be the last.

Baylor

After Princeton, we sold our home in southern California and moved to central Texas. I had accepted a tenure-track position at Baylor University as an Associate Professor of Church-State Studies, and Associate Director of the J. M. Dawson Institute of Church-State Studies. Soon after my arrival, some alumni at Baylor voiced objections to my hiring, since my views on church and state did not align with their understanding of the purpose of the Dawson Institute. Thankfully, that episode passed quickly. And the alumni with whom I would eventually work closely at Baylor have been more than welcoming and collegial. But even after that initial episode had passed, Baylor continued to be a tumultuous place for many of us, largely because there was a division among the faculty about the meaning and prospects of Baylor's "Vision 2012."

Vision 2012 is a 10-year blueprint, approved unanimously by the Board of Regents in the fall of 2001, to catapult Baylor into the top tier of American universities while maintaining its distinctively Christian identity. The Baylor president who had led the charge for the implementation of this vision, Robert B. Sloan, had been influenced by John Henry Cardinal Newman's *Idea of a University* (1852), in which Newman argued that if theology is knowledge, then a Christian university should treat it no differently than it treats other disciplines, such as chemistry, physics, English literature, or social work. Thus, to think of theology as merely personal and private—rising only slightly higher than matters of taste—excludes theology from the realm of "knowledge" and thus means it is likely to be taken less seriously than the other disciplines in the academy. The incoming provost, David Lyle Jeffrey, who participated in my interview for the position I was eventually offered, fully grasped this insight. He began the interview with this question, "Frank, we know you believe the Apostles' Creed. But my question to you is this: are those who don't believe the Apostles' Creed mistaken?" I thought to myself, "This guy gets it." The issue is *not* what I believe; the issue is whether I think my beliefs are *true*. Too often Christians, even very devout ones, believe either that the first entails the second or that the second is not relevant to a fully integrated understanding of the Christian faith. But in today's relativistic age, embracing either option aids and abets the enemies of the Gospel whether one intends to do so or not. This is what Pope Benedict XVI meant by the "dictatorship of relativism" in a homily he gave as Joseph

Cardinal Ratzinger soon after the death of John Paul II.[3] Baylor's incoming provost knew what he was doing.

It was only after I had begun at Baylor that I realized the greatness of David Jeffrey, who now serves as Distinguished Professor of Literature and Humanities in Baylor's Honors College. He is one of those people that you quickly realize has the sort of intellect that is the academic equivalent of Michael Jordan. As you might hear said of an extraordinary athlete on ESPN's Sportscenter, "You cannot stop him—you can only hope to contain him." An expert in medieval biblical hermeneutics and a variety of other areas of literary scholarship, he knows several languages, and late in his career he became involved with Chinese universities and so undertook to add Mandarin Chinese to his linguistic portfolio.

Over the years, David and his wife, Katherine, have become dear friends to both Frankie and me. When I was initially and controversially denied tenure in March 2006, David and Katherine were there for us, providing us with wonderful advice, listening ears, and prayerful encouragement.

Another courageous soul who helped me through my tenure case was C. Stephen Evans, University Professor of Philosophy and Humanities. Steve is a giant in Christian philosophy, and was one of my heroes while I was studying philosophy as an undergraduate and in graduate school. That hero status has not changed, and here is why.

Steve came to Baylor in 2002, leaving a well-regarded philosophy department at Calvin College. He, like many of us, was attracted to Baylor by Vision 2012 and its incredible promise for Christian scholarship. Steve's wife, Jan, is also a tenured professor at Baylor, teaching Spanish. Soon after I was denied tenure, Steve was so outraged that he told me in private conversation that if I did not win my appeal that he would consider resigning his prestigious university professorship. I was overwhelmed by this selfless charity, and I did not know what to say. It did not take long for Steve to make public what he had told me in private.[4] I am proud to say that I am now a colleague of Steve's since I moved from church-state studies to the philosophy department in June 2007. He, of course, still remains a hero of mine, and I do not anticipate that ever changing.

On September 22, 2006, Baylor University reversed its decision and awarded me tenure. And only 16 months after winning my appeal (in April 2008), I was promoted to full professor. In the academic world, such a story is as unlikely as they come. For this reason, I am in awe of, and humbled by, the gentle and unpredictable hand of providence that has taken my wife and me by its grace through one improbable scenario after another. Any success that I may have appeared to earn hangs by a thin string dangling from an intricate tapestry over a fiery abyss, whose creator is "the author and finisher of our faith" (Heb. 12:2 KJV).

When it comes to the bonds of Christian friendship, Baylor has been an embarrassment of riches for Frankie and me. In addition to those already mentioned, there are many, many others whom we think of as friends. And they consist of Catholics as well as Protestants from virtually every denomination.

Frankie's Father

Six weeks after I was denied tenure, my wife's father died. She adored him. And she pretty much was his main caregiver during his last months. I make mention of this because of how the death of my father-in-law, Joseph Alexander Dickerson Jr., intersected with our communion with the Catholic Church.

In the weeks following Joe's death, we discovered, among his personal items, a St. Christopher medal, inscribed "Bishop Choi to JD." It is our understanding that the bishop gave St. Christopher medals to pilots in the Pacific during World War II. Soon after the war, Joe, a pilot, joined the ROTC faculty at Fordham University. Impressed by the Jesuits there including the seriousness of their faith, Joe wanted to become Catholic, but my mother-in-law discouraged him. She told Joe that his parents would be devastated if he were to join the Catholic Church. So, Joe acquiesced to his wife and, as far as we know, never made a Christian commitment of any sort, though, ironically, he lived the Christian virtues better than most Christians. This is why when Frankie was received into the Catholic Church on August 18, 2007, she took the name "Joseph" as her Confirmation name, in honor of her father and his unfulfilled desire to become Catholic. For her confirmation gift I bought Frankie a St. Christopher medal with this inscription on the back, "From JAD to FRD."

In June 2006 while Frankie and I were attending an academic conference at a Hilton Hotel in Alexandria, Virginia, we noticed that my Baptist colleague Ralph C. Wood and his wife, Suzanne, were there as well. They greeted us at one of the elevators and we exchanged pleasantries. Ralph immediately noticed that something was wrong with Frankie. He inquired about her state of mind and soul. She took him aside and told him about the doubts she was experiencing about her father's posthumous fate. Ralph offered to Frankie a theological case for why he believed that her father would not be condemned to eternal separation from God. He told Frankie that her father's initial desire for full communion with the Catholic Church was an act of faith that God would honor. The Church calls such an act "the baptism of desire."[5] And given the Christian manner in which Joe had conducted his life since that time, as someone seemingly touched by God's grace, Ralph had no doubt that Joe is destined for an eternity with his Lord and Savior Jesus Christ. This gave Frankie much comfort.

After I had been received back into the Catholic Church and Frankie had become a candidate for reception, Ralph wrote the following to us in a May 7, 2007, email:

> *Dear Frankie & Frank:*
>
> *I wanted to add my own strong affirmation of your decision to be received into (and, in Frank's case returned to) the Roman Catholic Church.*
>
> *I'm sure you won't remember it, but at our very first meeting at a reception in President Sloan's home, I asked about Frank's upbringing. When you told me that you had been raised a Catholic, I immediately asked why you would leave a tradition so rich and deep? You replied that it had meant little to you as a youth and that your Christianity had come alive only through evangelical churches. I thus*

see your move, not as repudiating your evangelicalism
but rather as returning to its Catholic form. . . .

And as for you, dear Frankie, you were special to me from
the beginning of our friendship, and you have remained
so ever since. Our conversations last summer about your
father's death remain quite vivid to me, as I there learned that
your Christian faith runs very deep indeed. As with Frank,
I see this move as a further deepening of your witness. . . .

Several months after receiving this email from Ralph, something unusual happened to Frankie and me while we were over 700 miles apart. On Saturday, September 22, 2007, Frankie attended 6:00 p.m. Mass at St. Jerome's Catholic Church in Waco. As the people began receiving communion, she closed her eyes and saw Jesus at the table with his disciples at the Last Supper. But it was not the famous Leonardo DaVinci painting, for the characters were not still. In Frankie's vision, Jesus was in motion. She saw him talking and moving. Then all of a sudden, his beard and features became bright and expanded over the image in her mind's eye until everything was a bright white light. Communion occurred between 6:40 and 6:45 p.m.

Then after communion, during the time when everyone is quiet and still, Frankie had an image-type-thought of her Dad as a man in his 50s or 60s, in a full swing, teeing off at a golf course. And then she was flooded with a series of rapid thoughts, the realization, the clear impression, that the reason her Dad never went to the Protestant church with her Mom (and their four little girls) was because if he was going to go to church, it was going to be the Catholic Church or no place at all.

On that same evening of September 22, 2007, I was in Alabama at a Catholic Charismatic conference at Our Lady of Sorrows Catholic Church in the city of Homewood. I was there to give two invited talks, one of which was on my return to the Catholic Church. After my final talk, I sat alone in the church library working on some papers for my Baylor classes. Around 6:40 p.m., a woman I had met earlier in the day came into the library and asked if I would like to have a piece of "blessed bread." I asked her, "What's that?" She replied, "Well, my husband and I attend an Eastern rite Catholic Church, where he is a deacon. In our church, during the consecration of the bread, the priest leaves a portion of the loaf unconsecrated and then blesses the left over portion later. This is 'blessed bread.'" I had not heard of this practice. Nevertheless, I took a piece of the bread and ate it. We talked for a few minutes about a few theological matters. And then I told her about my wife's concern for her father's soul. I told this woman that he had wanted to become Catholic in the late 1940s and that my mother-in-law had strongly discouraged him from doing so. At this point, the woman's eyes began to well up with tears. She then told me that she believed that because God is good and merciful that he would honor my father-in-law's desire.

About an hour later, my wife and I talked on the cell phone. She told me about the vision that she had at St. Jerome's that evening. She told me that the images were vivid and the message was clear. Seeing the deacon's wife in the church parking lot heading for her car, I stopped her and shared with her what my wife had just told me over the phone. She again began to well up with tears and told me that above the altar where the bread was blessed at her church is a huge mural of the Last Supper, the same image seen in my wife's vision. So, while my wife had a vision of the Last Supper followed by vivid images of her father that conveyed to her a clear message of his desire to become Catholic, I had partaken of the bread that had been blessed under that mural of the Last Supper, which was followed by the assurance of a deacon's wife that God would honor my father-in-law's desire. I cannot help but believe that this provides us with hope that there is truly a communion of saints that includes my father-in-law.

5

Wisdom of My Ancestors

I mean to live my life an obedient man, but obedient to God, subservient to the wisdom of my ancestors; never to the authority of political truths arrived at yesterday at the voting booth.

William F. Buckley Jr.,
from *Up From Liberalism* (1959) [1]

And this one thing at least is certain; whatever history teaches, whatever it omits, whatever it exaggerates or extenuates, whatever it says and unsays, at least the Christianity of history is not Protestantism. If ever there were a safe truth, it is this. . . . To be deep in history is to cease to be a Protestant.

John Henry Cardinal Newman,
from *An Essay on the Development
of Christian Doctrine* (1845)[2]

On a spring evening in 2005, our phone rang and my wife answered it. She said, "Frank, it's your niece, Darby."
Let me explain Darby.

In 2005 she was an eight-year-old going on 30. She is one of those articulate little girls who is both precocious and mischievous. When her mother, Paige, nearly died of a brain tumor in 2004, Frankie and I had flown out to her home in northern Nevada to help out Darby's father, my brother Patrick, during Paige's recovery. In the afternoons, while Frankie took care of Darby's newborn sister and her elder sister was off somewhere reading, I played outside with Darby and her two other siblings. While I was pushing her sister and brother on the swings, Darby insisted that I play wiffleball with her. I told her that I would do so when I was finished at the swings. Darby would have none of that. She proceeded to fall down on the backyard grass, with plastic bat in hand, and began, with legs and arm flailing, to whine and cry like a wounded animal preparing to meet its Maker. I left the two children on the swings and walked over to the seemingly possessed Darby. I said, "That is the oldest trick in the book, sweetheart. It doesn't fool me, and it doesn't persuade me. In fact, I invented this trick. I think there's a place on the internet that will give you the whole history of the 'act like you need an exorcist until you get your way' tactic, and attributes its origin to my creative genius. So, it won't work with me. If you want me to play with you, be patient. But if you continue to act like a crazy girl, there will be no wiffleball." About fifteen minutes later Darby and I played wiffleball and we had a wonderful time. I tell this story because about a year later, Darby told her grandmother, in her articulate little voice, "Grandma Beckwith, Uncle Frank is the only person who really understands me."

Frankie handed me the phone. After pleasantries, Darby got down to business. "We were praying for you and Aunt Frankie at the dinner table this evening, and I was surprised to learn that you are not Catholic. That makes me very sad. Why aren't you and Aunt Frankie Catholic?" I proceeded to tell my little niece that I had great respect for the pope and that I have learned much from the Church's great thinkers, including Popes Benedict XVI and John Paul II. I also told her that I agree with most everything that the Catholic Church teaches on matters concerning God and Jesus, but I disagreed with it on other things having to do with the authority of the Church and the nature of communion and some of the other sacraments. (I had to remind myself I was talk-ing to a little girl, but with Darby you can easily forget.) After I was finished, there was a five second pause, and she said, "Okay. I understand. But I am still sad. We will pray for you." I said, "Put your father on the phone."

Her father, my brother Patrick, is seven years my junior. He is a Knights of Columbus Catholic, who, with his wife, teaches Natural Family Planning. He once actually wrote a letter to the Bishop of Las Vegas asking that a priest be reprimanded for allow-ing non-Catholics and divorced Catholics to receive communion at our nephew's First Holy Communion. On several occasions prior to my return to the Church, Patrick would have The Coming Home Network (a group dedicated to bringing ex-Catholics and Protestants into full communion with the Church) send me a nice card with a drawing of the Vatican on the front and an inscription that said something like, "You're always welcome in the Catholic Church."

When Patrick got on the phone I said, "What are you doing?" He said with a hint of mischief in his voice, "Look, she asked me why Uncle Frank and Aunt Frankie are not Catholic. I thought it would be wrong for me to speak for you. So, I said, 'Why don't you ask your Uncle Frank yourself?'"

This encounter with my niece marked the first step in our move-ment toward the Catholic Church. It seemed not to be such a big deal at the time. After all, this was an eight-year-old child unac-quainted with the serious theological questions for whom someone in my line of work requires answers. Although that may be true, beneath Darby's inquiry was a more fundamental question, one for which I should have had an answer: "Can I give a convincing account as to why I should permanently abandon the Church of my baptism?"

Slouching Toward Rome

After Darby's question, the next important encounter that helped propel me on my journey back to the Catholic Church occurred at a February 2006 conference on John Paul II and Philosophy, held at Boston College (BC).

Several months earlier I had published a small essay in the June 2005 issue of the magazine *Touchstone*: "Vatican Bible School: What John Paul II Can Teach Evangelicals." I incorporated portions of that essay in my conference paper. In a nutshell, I argued that Protestants who don't believe creeds are necessary—those who say things like "no creed but Christ"—do in fact accept creeds in the sense that they embrace fundamental doctrines that they believe are unassailable. Moreover, much of what these anti-creedal Protestants believe about Christ, the Trinity, the nature of scripture, and so forth are not easily derived from a reading of the Bible or a mere appeal to the words of Christ. Rather, they are beliefs that come from creeds and confessions that are the result of the hard work done by others in the first six centuries of the Christian Church. Thus, the reason why these anti-creedal Protestants can be so dismissive about creeds is that they do not appreciate how much of their own theology, including their anti-creedalism, is based on incorrigible truths that were formulated in creeds they claim are not necessary even as they implicitly accept them as normative. The anti-creedalist is like a rich nephew who finds himself with a full bank account, not knowing he inherited it from his uncle's fortune, but nevertheless claims to have earned it fair and square.

After I delivered my paper, the audience asked questions. The first question came from Laura Garcia, a BC philosophy professor and a former Evangelical Protestant who converted to Catholicism while in graduate school at the University of Notre Dame. She asked, "Your paper seems to imply the necessity of creeds in the first centuries of the Church. But that assumes the necessity of a Magisterium that has the authority to issue such creeds and declare them normative for all Christians. So, why aren't you a Catholic?" The question took me by surprise. After a brief pause, I gave her an answer—if I remember correctly—that first appealed to the chief doctrines of the Reformation as being Spirit-led correctives that reached back into the past to recover what the Roman Catholic Church had lost. By doing this, I tried to account for the church's continuity as being connected to the Reformers and their descendants as well as to their orthodox predecessors in the Catholic Church. In this way, I could defend the Catholic creeds as Spirit-directed without conceding the present authority of Rome on these matters. Ironically, I would later discover that the Catholic theologian (and convert from Lutheranism) Louis Bouyer offered a similar argument.[3] He correctly attributes Protestantism's spiritual virtues to the Reformers' recovery of, and reliance on, aspects of the Catholic tradition. However, unlike what I claimed at BC in 2006, Bouyer concluded that Luther and Calvin had unfortunately assimilated philosophical ideas that were deleterious to the Reformers' noble intent for the proper restoration of the Church. For this reason, the task of proper restoration fell to thoughtful Catholic reformers that led to the Council of Trent and its successors.

Though I believed I had escaped as an unscathed Protestant, the episode at BC piqued my interest in developing an understanding of the creeds that would not compel me to consider returning to Catholicism. I read several works including *Truth and Tolerance* (2004) and *Introduction to Christianity* (1990) by Joseph Cardinal Ratzinger (Pope Benedict XVI as of April 2005). Out of curiosity I also picked up David Currie's 1996 book, *Born Fundamentalist, Born-Again Catholic*. I was not entirely convinced by Currie's case, but he did raise some issues about the Early Church Fathers and the Catholic doctrines of the Eucharist and Infant Baptism that led me many months later to more scholarly sources that included J. N. D. Kelly's *Early Christian Doctrines* (1978).

At the time, though, I was most taken by the insights and compelling reasoning in Cardinal Ratzinger's *Truth and Tolerance*. There was much in this book that resonated with my own philosophical and theological interests and projects, especially as they touched on the issue of what it means to say that theology can yield knowledge. I even called my friend, the Evangelical Protestant philosopher J. P. Moreland, and read to him this paragraph from the book, without telling him its author:

"I am the way, and the truth, and the life": this saying of Jesus from the Gospel of John (John 14:6) expresses the basic claim of the Christian faith. The missionary tendency of this faith is based on that claim: Only if the Christian faith is truth does it concern all men; if it is merely a cultural variant of the religious experience of mankind that is locked up in symbols and can never be deciphered, then it has to remain within its own culture and leave others in theirs. That, however, means that the question about the truth is the essential question of the Christian faith as such, and in that sense it inevitably has to do with philosophy.[4]

I then asked J. P., "Guess who wrote this?" He reeled off the names of about three or four well-known Protestant theologians and philosophers. I said "no" after each name until he said, "Okay, I give up. Who is it?" I replied, "It's the Pope," to which he replied in exuberance, "He's one of us!"

A month after the Boston College conference I was denied tenure by Baylor University. Although, as recounted in the previous chapter, I eventually won my appeal, that victory did not occur until six months later. Besides the distractions of that battle and publicity surrounding it, I was preoccupied with personal and other professional matters. My father-in-law died, my mother had recently completed radiation and chemotherapy treatment following her mastectomy, and I was fully engaged in putting together the voluminous program for the Evangelical Theological Society meeting for the following November. So, I had to put my reading on the back burner until life at least began to resemble normality.

I Hear the Ancient Footsteps

Things had settled down by the fall of 2006. In late October, I lectured at the University of Dallas for the annual meeting of the Society of Catholic Social Scientists. I was asked to reply to a plenary address by J. Budziszewski, a friend who had been received into the Catholic Church three years earlier. J. is a professor of philosophy and government at the University of Texas in Austin. The morning after the lectures, my wife and I had breakfast with J. and his wife, Sandra. It must have lasted three hours. Although both of us asked J. and Sandra a lot of questions about Catholicism, it was Frankie who initiated the conversation and seemed far more animated than me in seeking answers.

Our questions focused on several theological issues that prevented us from becoming Catholic and seemed insurmountable: the doctrine of justification, the Real Presence in the Eucharist, the teaching authority of the Church (including apostolic succession and the primacy of the Pope), and Penance. The other issues that most Protestants find to be stumbling blocks—the Marian doctrines and Purgatory—were not a big deal to me. That was because I reasoned that if the Catholic views on Church authority, justification, the communion of the saints, and the sacraments were defensible, then these other so-called "stumbling blocks" withered away, since the Catholic Church would in fact be God's authoritative instrument in the development of Christian doctrine.

One may wonder where the Protestant doctrine of *sola scriptura* (or "scripture alone") factored in all this. To be blunt, it didn't, primarily because over the years I could not find an understanding or definition of *sola scriptura* convincing enough that did not have to be so qualified that it seemed to be more a slogan than a standard. Here is the way *sola scriptura* is defined in *The Westminster Confession of Faith* (1646):

> The whole counsel of God, concerning all things necessary for his own glory, man's salvation, faith and life, is either expressly set down in Scripture, or by good and necessary consequence may be deduced from Scripture: unto which nothing at any time is to be added, whether by new revelations of the Spirit or traditions of men.[5]

This was published long after the deaths of Martin Luther (1483–1546) and John Calvin (1509–64). The Reformation churches had been firmly established for many decades. It was a product of what has been called "Reformed scholasticism," and did not exhibit the more historically oriented understanding of *sola scriptura* that one finds in Luther and Calvin. As my Baptist Baylor colleague D. H. Williams points out, the "Magisterial Reformers such as Luther and Calvin did not think of *sola scriptura* as something that could be properly understood apart from the church or the foundational tradition of the church, even while they were opposing some of the institutions of the church."[6] This is why I found their *sola scriptura* views to be much more sensible than what I found among many contemporary Evangelical Protestants, who had imbibed far too much of the spirit of Reformed scholasticism. My Evangelical Protestant contemporaries seemed to treat the Bible as if it could be read as an authoritative depositary of orthodox doctrine apart from the historic church and the formation of Christian theology during the early centuries of its existence. The whole idea that, according to *The Westminster Confession*, one may "deduce" necessary doctrines from "scripture" treats theology as if it were a branch of mathematics. It's as if the Reformed scholastics were anticipating the nineteenth-century legal formalists of whom Oliver Wendell Holmes Jr. would write, "I once heard a very eminent judge say that he never let a decision go until he was absolutely sure that it was right. So judicial dissent often is blamed, as if it meant simply that one side or the other were not doing their sums right, and if they would take more trouble, agreement inevitably would come."[7]

But as I slowly and unconsciously moved toward Catholicism in the early 2000s, I began to even find the *sola scriptura* of the Magisterial Reformation not entirely satisfactory. It seemed to me to subtly and unconsciously incorporate into its theological framework all the doctrines that *sola scriptura,* without a settled canon or authoritative creedal tradition, could never have produced out of whole cloth without the benefit of a Holy Spirit-directed ecclesiastical infrastructure. It brought to mind what the philosopher Bertrand Russell said of the advantages of "the method of 'postulating'": "they are the same as the advantages of theft over honest toil."[8]

Many of the contemporary Evangelical Protestants I read offered understandings of *sola scriptura* that were based on less than convincing biblical exegesis,[9] or implicitly or explicitly relied on extra-scriptural support to justify either the scope of the biblical canon[10] or essential doctrines that are not easily derived from scripture without the necessary assistance of philosophical and theological categories arrived at through the development of doctrine that arose alongside, and in accordance with, the formation of the canon.[11] John Henry Cardinal Newman, for instance, asks us to consider just the doctrine of the Trinity as articulated in the Athanasian Creed developed in the late fourth century AD:

> Is this to be considered as a mere peculiarity or no? Apparently a peculiarity; for on the one hand it is not held by all Protestants, and next, it is not brought out in form in Scripture. First, the word Trinity is not in Scripture. Next I ask, *How* many of the verses of the Athanasian Creed are distinctly set down in Scripture? and further, take particular portions of the doctrine, viz., that Christ is co-eternal with the Father, that the Holy Ghost is God, or that the Holy Ghost proceedeth from the Father and the Son, and consider the kind of texts and the modes of using them, by which the proof is built up. Yet is there a more sacred, a more vital doctrine in the circle of the articles of faith than that of the Holy Trinity?[12]

In any event, I had for some time accepted a weak form of *sola scriptura*: any doctrine or practice inconsistent with scripture must be rejected, though it does not follow that any doctrine or practice not explicitly stated in scripture must suffer the same fate, for the doctrine or practice may be essential to Christian orthodoxy. This seemed to me to be the only defensible understanding of *sola scriptura*, though it certainly left much to be desired.

When Frankie and I entered into our conversation with J. and Sandra, I had some clear thoughts on the matters that divided Protestants and Catholics. As is his style, J. offered to Frankie and me eloquent answers, supported by thoughtful reasoning informed by his deep knowledge of history, philosophy, and the Bible. And Sandra contributed much to the conversation as well, offering to us important insights about her own internal deliberations that led her to the Catholic Church. At the end of the breakfast, J. strongly encouraged us to explore the Church Fathers as well as the *Catechism of the Catholic Church*.[13] I remained unmoved, though curious, given my own beliefs about the Catholic creeds and the role they played in the Church's use and understanding of scripture. I eventually did take J.'s advice, though it took several months for me to do so.

Ancient Footprints Everywhere

On November 17, 2006, I was elected the fifty-eighth president of the Evangelical Theological Society (ETS). I accepted this position of leadership while fully embracing a Protestant understanding on the four key issues I mentioned above: the doctrine of justification, the Real Presence in the Eucharist, the teaching authority of the Church (including apostolic succession and the primacy of the Pope), and Penance.

When we arrived at the conference hotel on the evening of November 14, we were greeted by many friends including Mark Foreman (a professor at Liberty University). Mark, who is a Reformed Episcopalian, joked with me about the paper I was set to deliver at the conference, "Faith, Reason, and the Christian University: What John Paul II Can Teach Evangelicals," a version of which I delivered at Boston College in 2006. Mark said, "When are you going to become Catholic?" I jokingly replied, "When my term as ETS president is over," though not seriously thinking I would ever return to the Catholic Church. I did share with Mark that I was very much attracted to Catholic views on faith and reason, moral theology, and the nature of the human person, but that there were some issues that were deal breakers (such as those mentioned above). I told Mark that it would probably take me many years to work these out, if I ever worked them out at all.

While at the 2006 conference in DC, I visited a bookstore by the hotel and purchased three small books authored by Joseph Cardinal Ratzinger (Pope Benedict XVI): *Christianity and the Crisis of Cultures* (2006), *In the Beginning* (1995), and *Values in a Time of Upheaval* (2006). I bought them because I was working on a new book on politics and Christianity and I wanted to glean from the Pope's insights on Christianity and culture. I read two of the three books on the flight home to Texas.

In early 2007, I followed J. Budziszewski's suggestion and began reading the early Church Fathers, focusing on the doctrines that were key for me.[14] I also dove into the *Catechism of the Catholic Church*, which is a marvelously readable presentation of Catholic beliefs. Included among the other works I consulted was *Is the Reformation Over? An Evangelical Assessment of Contemporary*

Roman Catholicism, authored by the eminent historian Mark A. Noll and journalist Carolyn Nystrom. Although this led me to read other sources, including the 1999 *Joint Declaration on the Doctrine of Justification by the Lutheran World Federation and the Catholic Church*,[15] I also read several reviews of the Noll/Nystrom book, one of which was written by Carl R. Trueman, Professor of Historical Theology and Church History at Westminster Theological Seminary. I single out this review because of its concluding paragraph, which rocked me to the core:

> When I finished reading the book, I have to confess that I agreed with the authors, in that it does indeed seem that the Reformation is over for large tracts of evangelicalism; yet the authors themselves do not draw the obvious conclusion from their own arguments. *Every year I tell my Reformation history class that Roman Catholicism is, at least in the West, the default position. Rome has a better claim to historical continuity and institutional unity than any Protestant denomination, let alone the strange hybrid that is evangelicalism; in the light of these facts, therefore, we need good, solid reasons for not being Catholic*; not being a Catholic should, in others words, be a positive act of will and commitment, something we need to get out of bed determined to do each and every day. *It would seem, however, that if Noll and Nystrom are correct, many who call themselves evangelical really lack any good reason for such an act of will; and the obvious conclusion, therefore, should be that they do the decent thing and rejoin the Roman Catholic Church.* I cannot go down that path myself, primarily because of my view of justification by faith and because of my ecclesiology; but those who reject the former and lack the latter have no real basis upon which to perpetuate what is, in effect, an act of schism on their part. For such, the Reformation is over; for me, the fat lady has yet to sing; in fact, I am not sure at this time that she has even left her dressing room.[16] (emphasis added)

Professor Trueman's reasoning would serve as a catalyst for reorienting my sense of whether the Catholic Church or I had the burden in justifying the schism in which I had remained for over thirty years.

I consulted numerous other sources, including a 1995 book authored by my dear friends Norm Geisler and Ralph MacKenzie, *Roman Catholics and Evangelicals: Agreements and Differences.* It is a fair-minded tome (though not without portions Catholics would challenge). But some of the points that Norm and Ralph make were really troubling. For example, in their section on salvation, they write: "Although the forensic aspect of justification stressed by Reformation theology is scarcely found prior to the Reformation, there is continuity between medieval Catholicism and the Reformers."[17] This idea, that the Reformation's view of forensic justification was a virtual theological innovation, is put forth even more strongly by none other than the great theologian and Oxford professor, Alister McGrath:

> The essential feature of the Reformation doctrines of justification is that a deliberate and systematic distinction is made between *justification* and *regeneration.* Although it must be emphasised that this distinction is purely notional, in that it is impossible to separate the two within the context of the *ordo salutis*, the essential point is that a notional distinction is made where none had been acknowledged before in the history of Christian doctrine. A fundamental discontinuity was introduced into western theological tradition where none had ever existed, or ever been contemplated, before. The Reformation understanding of the nature of justification—as opposed to its *mode*—must therefore be regarded as a genuine theological *novum.*[18]

What is the Reformed doctrine of forensic justification? It is the view that one is made right, or justified by God, as a consequence of God's gratuitously *imputing* to one Jesus's righteousness. By dying on the cross in our stead and thus for our sins, Jesus paid the price to God for the punishment we deserve, eternal separation from him. One is justified at the moment one accepts Christ at conversion. But this acceptance, an act of faith on the part of the believer, is itself the work of God. Thus, justification is entirely a consequence of God's grace. Accordingly, at conversion one is assured of salvation, for there is nothing that one can do or not do to lose or gain one's redemption.[19] But the grace one receives is legal or forensic. This means that grace is not real stuff that changes nature, but merely the name given to God's graciousness by legally accounting to us Christ's righteousness. This is why it is called the *imputation*, rather than an *infusion*, of God's grace. *Sanctification*, or as McGrath calls it, *regeneration*, is a consequence of one's conversion, the internal work of the Holy Spirit in one's Christian journey. Good works, the exercise of the Christian virtues, and the change in one's character over time are the natural outgrowth of one's justification. But justification and sanctification are different events, though the latter, which extends over the lifetime of the converted sinner, follows from the former in the life of the authentic Christian. Although McGrath maintains that the Reformed distinction between justification and regeneration is only notional, it is the understanding of justification as *exclusively* forensic that requires this notional distinction. Thus, even if the distinction is merely notional, the idea that required it, "the Reformed understanding of the nature of justification" (i.e., forensic justification), is, according to McGrath, "a genuine theological *novum*."

When I got around to reading the Church Fathers, the Reformation doctrine of justification was just not there, as Geisler, McKenzie, and McGrath candidly admit. To be sure, salvation by God's grace was there. To be sure, the necessity of faith was there as well. And to be sure, a believer's "works" apart from God's grace was decried. But what was present was a profound understanding of how saving faith was not a singular event that took place "on a Sunday," to quote a famous Gospel song. Rather, saving faith, entirely the consequence of God's grace, begins with one's initial conversion, which incorporates one into the family of God. But at that point the journey is just beginning. For one then exercises one's faith, itself a gift of God's grace, in acts of charity, the spiritual disciplines, and prayer as well as in the partaking of the sacraments—all this in order to commune with God to receive his unmerited grace to conform one into the image of Christ. According to this view, justification refers not only to the Christian's initial entrance into the family of God at baptism—which is administered for the remission of sins—but to the intrinsic work of both the infusion of that grace at baptism and all the subsequent graces that work in concert to transform the Christian from the inside out. It is in and through this ongoing transformation that one is made *justified*, in the same sense of being made righteous or rightly-ordered, and thus gifted to share in the divine life of Christ. Consequently, justification and sanctification are not different events, one extrinsic and the other intrinsic, as the Reformers taught. Rather, "sanctification" is the ongoing intrinsic work of justifying, or making rightly-ordered, the Christian by means of God's grace, the same grace that intrinsically changed the believer at the moment of her initial "justification" (i.e., at baptism) into an adopted child of the Father. For the Church Fathers, as it seems to me obvious from scripture (see chapter 6), justification is not only a matter of you getting into heaven, but also, and more importantly, a matter of getting heaven into you.[20] This, it turns out, is the view of justification taught in the *Catechism of the Catholic Church*.[21] It seemed to me that the chief distinction between the Protestant view of justification on the one hand, and the Catholic and Church Fathers' view on the other, rests on whether Christ's grace is infused or merely imputed at the moment one becomes a Christian at baptism and/or conversion.

At this juncture, I think it's important that the reader get a feel for how I read the Church Fathers and began to understand their views of grace and justification. I am going to first reproduce quotations from four of them that initially seem "Reformed," and are often cited as such by Protestant scholars.[22] These quotations will be followed by other quotations by the same four Fathers, though these latter ones do not sound Reformed at all. First, the apparently "Reformed" ones:

St. Irenaeus of Lyons (ca. AD 140–ca. AD 202)
> Vain, too, is [the effort of] Marcion and his followers when they [seek to] exclude Abraham from the inheritance, to whom the Spirit through many men, and now by Paul, bears witness, that "*he believed God, and it was imputed unto him for righteousness.*"[23]

St. Cyril of Jerusalem (ca. AD 318–AD 386)

For as a writing-reed or a dart has need of one to use it, so grace also has need of believing minds. . . . [I]t is God's to grant grace, but thine to receive and guard it.[24]

St. John Chrysostom (inter AD 344/354–AD 407)

In order then that the greatness of the benefits bestowed may not raise you too high, observe how he brings you down: "*by grace you have been saved*," says he, "*Through faith;*" Then, that, on the other hand, our free-will be not impaired, he adds also our part in the work, and yet again cancels it, and adds, "*And that not of ourselves.*"[25]

But this he calls God's righteousness, that from faith, because it comes entirely from the grace from above, and because men are justified in this case, not by labors, but by the gift of God.[26]

St. Augustine of Hippo (ca. AD 354–AD 430)

[Grace] is bestowed on us, not because we have done good works, but that we may be able to do them,—in other words, not because we have fulfilled the law, but in order that we may be able to fulfill the law.[27]

Now, if that's all one read from the Fathers, one may be led to think that the Reformation attempted to restore what the Church had once embraced, or at least implicitly held, from its earliest days. One would, of course, be partly right, since Luther did in fact correctly point out the contemporary abuses in Catholic practices that were inconsistent with the Gospel of grace, as some Catholic scholars have noted as well.[28] But a Gospel of grace, though clearly not contrary to the Reformed doctrine of justification, is also not contrary to the Catholic understanding of justification. This is why these *same Fathers* can also affirm particular beliefs and practices that a contemporary Protestant would think *inconsistent* with the Reformed doctrine of justification, but a Catholic would find perfectly consistent with her Church's view of justification. Here are those quotations, penned by the same Fathers quoted above:

St. Irenaeus of Lyons (ca. AD 140–ca. AD 202)

This able wrestler, therefore, exhorts us to the struggle for immortality, that we may be crowned, and may deem the crown precious, namely, that which is acquired by our struggle, but which does not encircle us of its own accord. And the harder we strive, so much is it the more valuable; while so much the more valuable it is, so much the more should we esteem it. And indeed those things are not esteemed so highly which come spontaneously, as those which are reached by much anxious care.[29]

St. Cyril of Jerusalem (ca. AD 318–AD 386)

For as a writing-reed or a dart has need of one to use it, so grace also has need of believing minds. You are receiving not a perishable but a spiritual shield. Henceforth you are planted in the invisible Paradise. Thou receivest a new name, which you had not before. Heretofore you were a Catechumen, but now you will be called a Believer. You are transplanted henceforth among the spiritual olive-trees, being grafted from the wild into the good olive-tree, from sins into righteousness, from pollutions into purity. You are made partaker of the Holy Vine. Well then, if thou abide in the Vine, you grow as a fruitful branch; but if thou abide not, you will be consumed by the fire. Let us therefore bear fruit worthily. God forbid that in us should be done what befell that barren fig-tree, that Jesus come not even now and curse us for our barrenness. But may all be able to use that other saying, But I am like a fruitful olive-tree in the house of God: I have trusted in the mercy of God for ever,—an olive-tree not to be perceived by sense, but by the mind, and full of light. As then it is His part to plant and to water, so it is thine to bear fruit: *it is God's to grant grace, but thine to receive and guard it.* Despise not the grace because it is freely given, but receive and treasure it devoutly.[30] (Italicized words are those of Cyril's quoted in the first set of the Fathers' quotes.)

Then, we pray [in the anaphora] for the holy fathers and bishops who have fallen asleep, and in general for all who have fallen asleep before us, in the belief that it is a great benefit to the souls on whose behalf the supplication is offered, while the holy and tremendous Victim is present. . . . By offering to God our supplications for those who have fallen asleep, if they have sinned, we . . . offer Christ sacrificed for the sins of all, and so render favorable, for them and for us, the God who loves man.[31]

St. John Chrysostom (inter AD 344/354–AD 407)

Let us then give them aid and perform commemoration for them. For if the children of Job were purged by the sacrifice of their father, why do you doubt that when we too offer for the departed, some consolation arises to them? [For] God is wont to grant the petitions of those who ask for others. And this Paul signified saying, that in a manifold Person your gift towards us bestowed by many may be acknowledged with thanksgiving on your behalf (2 Cor. i. 11.). Let us not then be weary in giving aid to the departed, both by offering on their behalf and obtaining prayers for them: for the common Expiation of the world is even before us.[32]

Mourn for those who have died in wealth, and did not from their wealth think of any solace for their soul, who had power to wash away their sins and would not. Let us all weep for these in private and in public, but with propriety, with gravity, not so as to make exhibitions of ourselves; let us weep for these, not one day, or two, but all our life. Such tears spring not from senseless passion, but from true affection. The other sort are of senseless passion. For this cause they are quickly quenched, whereas if they spring from the fear of God, they always abide with us. Let us weep for these; let us assist them according to our power; let us think of some assistance for them, small though it be, yet still let us assist them. How and in what way? By praying and entreating others to make prayers for them, by continually giving to the poor on their behalf.[33]

St. Augustine of Hippo (ca. AD 354–AD 430)

> We run, therefore, whenever we make advance; and our whole-
> ness runs with us in our advance (just as a sore is said to
> run when the wound is in process of a sound and careful
> treatment), in order that we may be in every respect perfect,
> without any infirmity of sin whatever result which God not
> only wishes, but even causes and helps us to accomplish.
> And this God's grace does, in co-operation with ourselves,
> through Jesus Christ our Lord, as well by commandments,
> sacraments, and examples, as by His Holy Spirit also; through
> whom there is hiddenly shed abroad in our hearts . . . that
> love, "which makes intercession for us with groanings which
> cannot be uttered," . . . until wholeness and salvation be per-
> fected in us, and God be manifested to us as He will be seen
> in His eternal truth.[34]

For a Catholic, these two sets of quotations from the Fathers
are perfectly consistent with each other, since an inconsistency
only arises if one first embraces a Reformed view of imputed righteousness as well as its distinction between justification and sanctification. Some specific points from these quotes are worth singling
out. John Chrysostom, for instance, writes of praying for the dead
so that the living through their prayers and charity may affect the
dead's purification in the afterlife. (This is what the Church calls
the "doctrine of purgatory," which is merely an extension of the
biblical doctrine of sanctification;[35] see note 36.) This is reinforced
by Cyril's description of the Catholic Mass in which prayers are
said for deceased bishops and fellow believers, because these prayers
are "a great benefit to the souls on whose behalf the supplication
is offered, while the holy and tremendous Victim [Christ's body
and blood in the Eucharist] is present."

These comments by both John and Cyril are consistent with
the *Catholic Catechism*[36] and found deep in Christian history,[37]
and thus it is not surprising that "all the ancient liturgies included
prayers commemorating the 'faithful departed'. . . . [who] were
not simply remembered, they were welcomed as participants in
the liturgy."[38]

Cyril explains justification by the metaphor of being grafted onto a vine, bearing fruit, and continuing to abide in the vine, though he warns of the possibility of our ceasing to abide and being "consumed by the fire." And yet, Cyril clearly affirms that one's abiding is the result of grace "freely given" and that one should "receive and guard it" and "treasure it devoutly," which implies the believer's lifelong cooperation in justification. Irenaeus refers to "the struggle for immortality" as a "crown" for which "we strive." Augustine echoes Irenaeus and Cyril when he speaks of our moving toward perfection by God's grace through Jesus Christ and "by the commandments, sacraments, and examples, as by His Holy Spirit."

The beautiful articulation of God's grace that one finds in these Fathers, in both sets of quotations, is elegantly tied together in the account of grace and merit that one finds in the *Catechism of the Catholic Church*:

> The merit of man before God in the Christian life arises from the fact that *God has freely chosen to associate man with the work of his grace*. The fatherly action of God is first on his own initiative, and then follows man's free acting through his collaboration, so that the merit of good works is to be attributed in the first place to the grace of God, then to the faithful. Man's merit, moreover, itself is due to God, for his good actions proceed in Christ, from the predispositions and assistance given by the Holy Spirit.[39]

My study of the Fathers led me to reexamine the Canons of the Council of Orange (AD 529), which, with papal sanction, rejected as heretical Pelagianism and semi-Pelagianism. Having its origin in the Catholic monk Pelagius (ca. 354–ca. 420/440), the first heresy affirms that human beings do not inherit Adam's sin (and thus denies the doctrine of original sin) and by their free will may achieve salvation without God's grace. On the other hand, semi-Pelagianism maintains that a human being, though weakened by original sin, may make the initial act of will toward achieving salvation prior to receiving the necessary assistance of God's grace. The Council of Orange, in contrast, argued that Adam's original sin is inherited by his progeny and can be removed only by the sacrament of Baptism.

By the means of Baptism God's unmerited grace is infused for the remission of sins. Then the Christian's sanctification continues throughout his lifetime, entirely the work of the infusion of grace with which the Christian cooperates,[40] for the Christian "does nothing good for which God is not responsible, so as to let him do it."[41] Even though Protestant thinkers sometimes portray the Council of Orange's canons as a sort of paleo-Reformed document,[42] it is the Reformation notion of imputed righteousness that, ironically, puts the Reformers partially in the Pelagian camp. This is because the Reformers and Pelagians agree that God's *infused* grace is not necessary for justification.

Of course, some Church Fathers disagreed with each other on a variety of matters, and some of them in fact defended positions that were later declared heretical by Church Councils.[43] But it is interesting to note that on the question of the *correctness* of the doctrines and practices over which contemporary Evangelical Protestants and Catholics generally divide—the Real Presence of the Eucharist, apostolic succession, prayers for and to the dead, penance, infusion of grace, etc.—one does not find in the Fathers warring camps with one risking an ecumenical council's judgment of heresy, as in the Arian and Pelagian controversies. In fact, for the Fathers the correctness of the "Catholic" doctrines and practices seem conspicuously *uncontroversial*. To be sure, one finds among the Fathers different degrees of emphasis on some of these matters and how best to understand them and conceptualize them. The fourth century Donatists, for example, denied the efficaciousness of sacraments administered by bad ministers (e.g., apostate bishops, those that denied the faith during persecution and then returned, etc.), but they did not object to the notion of a sacrament being an efficacious means of grace per se. This error led Augustine to develop the *ex opere operato* teaching on the sacraments, which is the present doctrine of the Catholic Church.[44] To cite another example: some Fathers explicitly assert the primacy of the Bishop of Rome, while others seem to articulate an understanding of the episcopate that offers some hints but little clarity on the question of primacy. But what is not in dispute is that none of the Fathers either denies apostolic succession or unequivocally affirms a Free Church understanding of church government.[45] I mention this because I had thought for some time that if I could, for example, show that Church Father X asserted the primacy of Rome and Church Father Y did not do so, then the case for apostolic succession is weakened and I have yet another reason not to move Romeward. But, when I ceased reading the Fathers anachronistically, what I began to notice was the far more important fact that Church Fathers X and Y agreed that without apostolic succession there is no Church, and that no Father implies or affirms that apostolic succession is a non-Christian view. Thus, one of the great ironies of my journey is that I would sometimes inadvertently draw conclusions that made the general case for Catholicism far more plausible in my mind than the particular Protestant doctrine for which I was arguing.

6

Every Word a Little Branch

For some years now I have read through the Bible twice every year. If you picture the Bible to be a mighty tree and every word a little branch, I have shaken every one of these branches because I wanted to know what it was and what it meant.

Martin Luther (1532) [1]

I am the true vine, and my Father is the vinegrower. He removes every branch in me that bears no fruit. Every branch that bears fruit he prunes to make it bear more fruit. You have already been cleansed by the word that I have spoken to you. Abide in me as I abide in you. Just as the branch cannot bear fruit by itself unless it abides in the vine, neither can you unless you abide in me. I am the vine, you are the branches.

Jesus of Nazareth (John 15:1–5a NRSV)

The fatal metaphor of progress, which means leaving things behind us, has utterly obscured the real idea of growth, which means leaving things inside us.

G. K. Chesterton,
from "The Romance of Rhyme" (1923) [2]

Although it had become clear to me that the Church Fathers were far more Catholic than they were Protestant, I needed to be convinced that their views on justification were consistent with scripture. I also had to be convinced that the "Catholic practices" that were impediments for me—the Real Presence in the Eucharist, the teaching authority of the Church (including apostolic succession and the primacy of the Pope), and Penance—were legitimate Christian beliefs and practices with long orthodox histories. It did not take long to be persuaded.

What the Scriptures Tell

As I more deeply delved into the issue of justification, I was struck by how the Catholic view seamlessly tied together the teachings of Jesus with the teachings of the New Testament found outside the Gospels. It is a testimony to the hegemonic influence of the Reformation's reading of Paul's epistles, and its assumed canonical and interpretative priority, that forensic justification colors every apparently contrary text with which I had come in contact during my Protestant days. (I call this "methodological Protestantism.") It is no wonder, then, that it was only when I began to reconsider Catholicism that I consulted, with an openness to be corrected, the teachings of Jesus, the larger context in which the Pauline Protestant proof-texts rested, and those New Testament passages that seemed "Catholic" but were often "reinterpreted" to fit the Reformed theological system.

I'm not suggesting, of course, that it is impermissible for theologians to offer interpretations of problematic passages in order to show that these passages are in fact consistent with other passages about which the scholar is more certain. We all do that. For it is the nature of an active mind to try to show that one's view, in whatever discipline, accounts for the most facts and has the least problems in comparison to its rivals. This is why I do not think that the Reformed Protestant view of justification is obviously unreasonable or that one cannot make a biblical case for it that some will find persuasive. Some of the brightest people I know are Reformed theologians, and I have great respect for the work they do. But what I am suggesting is that for me, all things considered, the Catholic view has more explanatory power than the Protestant view. This is why it made sense to me that the Early Church Fathers, as I noted in chapter 5, were so Catholic in their teachings. They held to a view that, I believe, does the best job of accounting for *all* the New Testament's passages on justification and sanctification.

So, I will offer a brief account of how I became convinced that the Catholic position has the most explanatory power to account for all of the New Testament's presentations of salvation. Of course, I know that some of my readers will not see these passages the way I have come to see them. But my purpose is not to offer a sophisticated apologetic for the Catholic view. Rather, I am just trying to communicate, as best I can, the internal deliberations that convinced me that I ought to embrace it.

The Teachings of Jesus

Once I ceased approaching the biblical text with methodological Protestantism, it was nearly impossible for me to get forensic justification from the teachings of Jesus. At the Last Judgment, for example, the difference between the sheep and the goats is between what they did and did not *do* (Matt. 25:31–46). There is no indication that Jesus is thinking of the sheep's "works" as "evidence of justification." But rather, these works serve in some way as the *basis on which* his judgment of their eternal fate is made. It would be absurd, for example, for a judge in a court of law to tell a guilty defendant that his guilt was not based on the defendant's actual deeds for which he was being prosecuted, but rather because the deeds are evidence of the guilt he had before he had actually engaged in the deeds.[3]

Jesus tells his disciples in Matthew 16:27, "For the Son of man is to come with his angels in the glory of his Father, *and then he will repay every man for what he has done*" (emphasis added). In Revelation 22:11–12, John quotes Jesus as saying, "Let the evildoer still do evil, and the filthy still be filthy, and the righteous still do right, and the holy still be holy. Behold, I am coming soon, *bringing my recompense, to repay every one for what he has done"* (emphasis added). In Matthew 19, Jesus connects the possession of eternal life (or salvation) with keeping the commandments, selling everything one owns (as he applied it to his questioner), and leaving everything including one's family if necessary.

Couple these with Matthew 5, and the richness of Jesus's teachings on salvation comes out even clearer:

> In the same way, every good tree bears good fruit, but the bad tree bears bad fruit. A good tree cannot bear bad fruit, nor can a bad tree bear good fruit. Every tree that does not bear good fruit is cut down and thrown into the fire. Thus you will know them by their fruits. *Not everyone who says to me, "Lord, Lord," will enter the kingdom of heaven, but only the one who does the will of my Father in heaven.* On that day many will say to me, "Lord, Lord, did we not prophesy in your name, and cast out demons in your name, and do many deeds of power in your name?" Then I will declare to them, "I never knew you; go away from me, you evildoers." *Everyone then who hears these words of mine and acts on them* will be like a wise man who built his house on rock. The rain fell, the floods came, and the winds blew and beat on that house, but it did not fall, because it had been founded on rock. And everyone who hears these words of mine and does not act on them will be like a foolish man who built his house on sand. The rain fell, and the floods came, and the winds blew and beat against that house, and it fell—and great was its fall! (Matt. 7:17–27 NRSV, emphasis added)

It is the bearing of fruit, the hearing and *acting on* Christ's words, the *doing the will of his Father* that constitute the life of faith, a life likened by Jesus to a house that *could fall* if not adequately constructed to withstand severe adversity. In John 14, Jesus tells his followers a bit of what it will mean when he says, "because I live, you will live also" (John 14:19). He states, "In that day you will know that I am in my Father, and you in me, and I in you. *He who has my commandments and keeps them, he it is who loves me*; and he who loves me will be loved by my Father, and I will love him and manifest myself to him" (John 14:20–21). The Gospel of Mark recounts these words of Christ, "If any man would come after me, *let him deny himself and take up his cross and follow me*. For whoever would save his life will lose it; and whoever loses his life for my sake and the gospel's will save it" (Mark 8:34b–35). In Mark 4, Jesus explains the parable of the seeds in which he tells his listeners of those who receive the word "with joy," but it has "no root" and thus "they fall away" immediately "when trouble or persecution arises" (Mark 4:16–17 NRSV). He also tells of "the ones sown on the good soil: *they hear the word and accept it and bear fruit*, thirty and sixty and a hundredfold" (Mark 4:20 NRSV).[4]

Mere imputed righteousness seems like the furthest idea from what one finds in these and other sayings of Jesus. What one finds is an active faith by which God's grace gives us new life (not just new status), and therefore there is a responsibility of obedience on our part to remain faithful, bear fruit, practice charity, and persevere. It is only later in the Pauline and non-Pauline Epistles—as the Church's doctrines begin to develop—that the people of God receive clarification on the role of God's grace in the life of Christian obedience. This is what I call *the journey of justification*.

The Journey of Justification

Consider first, Romans 4:1–8, often cited by Protestant authors as the definitive verse establishing the forensic doctrine of justification:

> What then are we to say was gained by Abraham, our ancestor according to the flesh? For if Abraham was justified by works, he has something to boast about, but not before God. For what does the scripture say? "Abraham believed God, and it was reckoned to him as righteousness." Now to one who works, wages are not reckoned as a gift but as something due. But to one who without works trusts him who justifies the ungodly, such faith is reckoned as righteousness. So also David speaks of the blessedness of those to whom God reckons righteousness apart from works: "Blessed are those whose iniquities are forgiven, and whose sins are covered; blessed is the one against whom the Lord will not reckon sin." (Rom. 4:1–8 NRSV)

The Reformed interpretation of this passage is that Paul is teaching that Christ's righteousness is imputed to us because of our faith in Christ, just as God reckoned Abraham as righteous because of his faith in God. Because the reckoning is a gift and thus not something owed or earned, the imputed righteousness received by the believer cannot be the consequence of the believer's works. That is all true, *if* the totality of justification is mere imputed righteousness. But the passage does not say that, and the other works of Paul's, as well as the writings of other New Testament authors, does not say it either.

If one looks at the wider context of Romans, what Paul seems to be saying in chapter 4 is that the works of the Mosaic law do not forensically justify, in the sense that one can accumulate enough works in order to please God, just as one would raise enough cash in order to pay off a debt to a creditor. Remember that the context of Romans concerns the relationship between Jewish and Gentile Christians, the former of which were suggesting to their Gentile brethren that obedience to the Mosaic law—especially circumcision—was a necessary condition for entrance into the Body of Christ. When Paul writes of "works" in the context of Romans 4 he is writing about the requirements of the Mosaic Law (or "works of the law"), including circumcision. He is not denigrating works per se, as we shall see below. He is, in fact, criticizing those who see obedience to the Mosaic Law as earning the salvation which God will owe them as a reward for their works. But that's not the Christian Gospel.

There is no doubt that Abraham was reckoned righteous precisely because he acted in faith. But Romans 4 does not say whether this is a once-and-for-all forensic imputation of righteousness, which is the Protestant view. For the scriptural quote in verse 3—"Abraham believed God, and it was reckoned to him as righteousness"—is from Genesis 15:6, in which we are told that Abraham believed God after the Lord had promised him numerous descendants. Yet, James 2:21–24 states that Abraham's faith justified him years after that incident when he obeyed God and attempted to offer his son Isaac as a sacrifice (Gen. 22:1–19). The text claims that when Abraham performed this work "the scripture was fulfilled which says, 'Abraham believed God, and it was reckoned to him as righteousness'; and he was called the friend of God" (James 2:23). However, the book of Hebrews teaches that Abraham was a man of faith in

Genesis 12, chronologically prior to the incidents referenced in Romans (Gen. 15) and James (Gen. 22): "By faith Abraham obeyed when he was called to go out to a place which he was to receive as an inheritance; and he went out, not knowing where he was to go" (Heb. 11:8). As Richard A. White writes:

> Thus, Gen. 15 could not be Abraham's conversion experience, as many Protestants contend, though he was justified then. On the other hand, the passage conforms quite well to the Catholic idea of progressive justification. Justification, though momentary when one first receives it through Baptism, is also progressive. It is the life of the child of God maturing in God's grace. Abraham was in God's favor as far back as Gen. 12, even though he is "declared righteous" in Gen. 15.[5]

Thus, it seemed clear to me that in order for it to be unreasonable for one to dispute the Protestant interpretation of Romans 4, the text would have to unequivocally state that Abraham was reckoned righteous at one decisive moment *and yet remained* inherently unrighteous, which is the Protestant doctrine of forensic justification. But it does not say that. Consider this example. If a jury declared Fred not guilty, it would not logically follow that it was also declaring that Fred is inherently innocent, though he in fact *may be* inherently innocent. Nothing, therefore, about a defendant's inner state of being (whether he is in *reality* innocent) follows from the legal declaration of his innocence. Thus, if Fred were to become inherently righteous as a consequence of an intrinsic change in him because of God's infused grace, a just God would have warrant to also legally *declare* him righteous.[6]

So, then, the real question is whether Paul and the other non-Gospel New Testament authors teach that *the entirety of justification is mere imputed righteousness that occurs once and for all.* The answer at which I arrived was "no." The following is a brief encapsulation of my reasoning, which unfolded and crystallized over a several-month period of reading and reflection.

In Romans 5:19, Paul writes, "For as by one man's disobedience many were *made sinners*, so by one man's obedience many will be *made righteous.*" If Adam's sin had real ontological consequences for human nature—"many were made sinners"—as this passage clearly indicates, then Jesus's death and resurrection has real ontological consequences as well—"many will be made righteous." It seems, then, that original sin and infused grace are a package deal. This is why it seems to me that Paul can sternly reject the value of works for justification apart from one's becoming a "new creation": "For in Christ Jesus *you are all sons of God,* through faith. For as many of you as were baptized into Christ have put on Christ" (Gal. 3:26–27). "For in Christ Jesus neither circumcision nor uncircumcision is of any avail, *but faith working through love*" (Gal. 5:6). "For neither circumcision counts for anything, nor uncircumcision, but *a new creation*" (Gal. 6:15).[7]

Although Paul certainly refers to justification as a past event (Rom. 5:1–2; 5:9; 8:24; 1 Cor. 6:11), he also presents it as a continuing process (1 Cor. 1:18; 15:2; 2 Cor. 2:15), as well as one that has not been fully achieved (Rom. 2:13; Gal. 5:5; 1 Cor. 3:15; 5:5; 1 Tim. 2:15; 2 Tim. 4:8, 18).

Moreover, works done in faith by God's grace contribute to our inward transformation and eventual justification. Paul writes in Romans 2:

> [God] will render to every man according to his works: to those who by patience in well-doing seek for glory and honor and immortality, he will give eternal life; but for those who are factious and do not obey the truth, but obey wickedness, there will be wrath and fury. There will be tribulation and distress for every human being who does evil, the Jew first and also the Greek, but glory and honor and peace for everyone who does good, the Jew first and also the Greek. . . . For it is not the hearers of the law who are righteous before God, but the doers of the law who will be justified. (Rom. 2:6–10, 13, emphasis added)

Paul writes to the Colossians that Christ "has now reconciled" them "in his body of flesh by his death, in order to present [them] holy and blameless and irreproachable before him, *provided that [they] continue in the faith, stable and steadfast*, not shifting from the hope of the gospel which [they] heard, which has been preached to every creature under heaven, and of which I, Paul, became a minister" (Col. 1:22–23). Paul tells the Philippians to *"work out your own salvation* with fear and trembling; *for God is at work in you*, both to will and to work for his good pleasure" (Phil. 2:12–13). He teaches the Galatians that "he who sows to his own flesh will from the flesh reap corruption; but *he who sows to the Spirit will from the Spirit reap eternal life*" (Gal. 6:8). In his second letter to Timothy, Paul writes "I have fought the good fight, I have finished the race, *I have kept the faith*," and consequently, *"there is laid up for me the crown of righteousness*, which the Lord, the righteous judge, *will award to me* on that Day, and not only to me *but also to all who have loved his appearing*" (2 Tim. 4:7–8). In this passage final justification is awarded for keeping the faith and persevering, but these are connected to a certain sort of inward change, the love for Christ's appearing.[8]

Thus, one does not find in Paul the sharp distinction between justification and sanctification that one finds among Reformed writers. In fact, the passages we have covered seem to indicate that justification *includes* sanctification. Here are a few others from the Pauline corpus that seem to support this understanding as well:[9]

And such were some of you. But *you were washed, you were sanctified, you were justified* in the name of the Lord Jesus Christ and in the Spirit of our God. (1 Cor. 6:11)

But we are bound to give thanks to God always for you, brethren beloved by the Lord, *because God chose you from the beginning to be saved, through sanctification by the Spirit* and belief in the truth. (2 Thess. 2:13)

For God has done what the law, weakened by the flesh, could not do: sending his own Son in the likeness of sinful flesh and for sin, he condemned sin in the flesh, *in order that the just requirement of the law might be fulfilled in us, who walk not according to the flesh but according to the Spirit.* (Rom. 8:3–4)

[God] saved us, not because of deeds done by us in righteousness, but in virtue of his own mercy, *by the washing of regeneration and renewal in the Holy Spirit*, which he poured out upon us richly through Jesus Christ our Savior, *so that we might be justified by*

his grace and become heirs in hope of eternal life. The saying is
sure. I desire you to insist on these things, *so that those who have
believed in God may be careful to apply themselves to good deeds;
these are excellent and profitable to men.* (Titus 3:5–8)

I am speaking in human terms, because of your natural limitations.
For just as you once yielded your members to impurity and to greater
and greater iniquity, *so now yield your members to righteousness for
sanctification.* When you were slaves of sin, you were free in regard
to righteousness. But then what return did you get from the things of
which you are now ashamed? The end of those things is death. *But
now that you have been set free from sin and have become slaves
of God, the return you get is sanctification and its end, eternal life.*
For the wages of sin is death, but the free gift of God is eternal life
in Christ Jesus our Lord. (Rom. 6:19–23)

What about other New Testament writers? In James 2 we are
told that justification is *not* by faith alone once and for all:

So faith by itself, if it has no works, is dead. But some one will say,
"You have faith and I have works." Show me your faith apart from
your works, and I by my works will show you my faith. You believe
that God is one; you do well. Even the demons believe—and shudder.
Do you want to be shown, you shallow man, that faith apart from
works is barren? Was not Abraham our father justified by works,
when he offered his son Isaac upon the altar? You see that faith was
active along with his works, and faith was completed by works, and
the scripture was fulfilled which says, "Abraham believed God, and
it was reckoned to him as righteousness"; and he was called the
friend of God. You see that a man is justified by works and not by
faith alone. (James 2:17–24)

Some Protestant writers claim that this passage from James is
not inconsistent with forensic justification, since the works spoken
of here are the effect of the cause of saving faith.[10] But, as Baptist
New Testament scholar Paul Rainbow points out, "In vain do we
search in James 2:14–26 for any statement of a causal relationship
between faith and works or between righteousness and obedience.
What jumps out from the material is a thrice-stated avowal of the
instrumentality of justification, that is 'by works'. . . ."[11] Other

Protestant writers argue that James is addressing the public display of one's salvation by one's works in order to show evidence of one's salvation, that is, to "justify" it in front of others.[12] But that's an implausible reading, since James's focus is clearly on God's justification of the Christian and not on public displays of righteousness. After all, the story of Abraham and Isaac occurred in a place isolated from the general public. Rainbow correctly points out that "the drift of the passage is to present human beings before God in good favor."[13]

It seems to me that James is indeed a problem if one maintains a forensic view of justification. But if one brackets that view and opens oneself to the Catholic view—that justification is the result of infused rather than imputed grace—then one need not think of "works" as activities by which one earns heaven as if one were appeasing a creditor in a debtors prison. Rather, a Christian's good works are performed in order that the grace that God has given us may be lived out so that we may become more like Christ. As I have said, the purpose of "good works" for the Catholic is not to get you into heaven, but to get heaven into you.[14] The Catholic already believes that he or she is an adopted child of God wholly by God's grace.[15] For the practicing Catholic, good works, including participating in the sacraments, works of charity, and prayer, are *not* for the purpose of earning heaven. For good works are not meant to pay off a debt in the Catholic scheme of things. Rather, good works prepare us for heaven by shaping our character and keeping us in communion with God so that we may be "holy and blameless and irreproachable before him" (Col. 1:22).

We might say that Paul, the most "systematic" of New Testament authors, most keenly and distinctly lays out the relationship between grace, faith, works, and salvation, as when he tells the Philippians (in a passage already quoted) to "*work out your own salvation* with fear and trembling; *for God is at work in you*, both to will and to work for his good pleasure" (Phil. 2:12–13, emphasis added). But this teaching is present not only in the Gospels and epistles of Paul and James; it is found elsewhere in the New Testament. Consider just these few (but representative) samples:[16]

So Jesus also suffered outside the gate *in order to sanctify the people through his own blood*. (Heb. 13:12)

And by that will *we have been sanctified through the offering of the body of Jesus Christ once for all*. And every priest stands daily at his service, offering repeatedly the same sacrifices, which can never take away sins. But when Christ had offered for all time a single sacrifice for sins, he sat down at the right hand of God, then to wait until his enemies should be made a stool for his feet. *For by a single offering he has perfected for all time those who are being sanctified*. (Heb. 10:10–14)[17]

Peter, an apostle of Jesus Christ, To the exiles of the Dispersion in Pontus, Galatia, Cappadocia, Asia, and Bithynia, *chosen and destined by God the Father and sanctified by the Spirit for obedience to Jesus Christ* and for sprinkling with his blood: *May grace and peace be multiplied to you*. Blessed be the God and Father of our Lord Jesus Christ! By his great mercy we have been *born anew to a living hope* through the resurrection of Jesus Christ from the dead, and to an inheritance which is imperishable, undefiled, and unfading, kept in heaven for you. (1 Pet. 1:1–4)

And I said, "Who are you, Lord?" And the Lord said, "I am Jesus whom you are persecuting. But rise and stand upon your feet; for I have appeared to you for this purpose, to appoint you to serve and bear witness to the things in which you have seen me and to those in which I will appear to you, delivering you from the people and from the Gentiles—to whom I send you to open their eyes, that they may turn from darkness to light and from the power of Satan to God, *that they may receive forgiveness of sins and a place among those who are sanctified by faith in me*." (Acts 26:15–18)

Once I abandoned methodological Protestantism, I could not find the substance of the Reformed view of justification in my reading of the New Testament without artificially forcing the text into Protestant categories. To be sure, I was fully aware how Protestant theologians made their case, and I was capable of following their reasoning. But I no longer found their case convincing. Moreover, the Reformed distinction between justification and sanctification, though seemingly defensible in light of certain biblical texts when isolated and explained by Reformed theologians, just could not be sustained in light of the entirety of the New Testament canon. Add to this the historical novelty of the Reformed doctrine of forensic justification as well as the development of sacraments, practices, and doctrines in both the Eastern and Western Churches that were totally oblivious to the Reformed view, and it seemed to me that Protestantism's view of justification had an enormous burden that it could not meet.

Robert Wilken writes that "any effort to mount an interpretation of the Bible that ignores its first readers is doomed to end up with a bouquet of fragments that are neither the book of the church nor the imaginative wellspring of Western literature, art and music. Uprooted from the soil that feeds them, they are like cut flowers whose vivid colors have faded."[18] Thus, it did not surprise me that when I read the *Catechism of the Catholic Church* it seemed to tie together the scriptures and the Church Fathers in a far more elegant, rich, multilayered, and convincing way than could any Protestant account. Although I have already quoted from the *Catechism* several times, I believe it is important to now quote portions of it on the topic of justification so that the reader will better understand why I came to the conclusion that the Catholic view has more explanatory power in accounting for what I found both in the Bible and in the Early Church:

> The first work of the grace of the Holy Spirit is conversion, effecting justification in accordance with Jesus' proclamation at the beginning of the Gospel: "Repent, for the kingdom of heaven is at hand." Moved by grace, man turns toward God and away from sin, thus accepting forgiveness and righteousness from on high. "Justification is not only the remission of sins, but also the sanctification and renewal of the interior man."
>
> Justification detaches man from sin which contradicts the love of God, and purifies his heart of sin. Justification follows upon God's merciful initiative of offering forgiveness. It reconciles man with God. It frees from the enslavement to sin, and it heals.
>
> Justification is at the same time the acceptance of God's righteousness through faith in Jesus Christ. Righteousness (or "justice") here means the rectitude of divine love. With justification, faith,

hope, and charity are poured into our hearts, and obedience to the divine will is granted us.

Justification has been merited for us by the Passion of Christ who offered himself on the cross as a living victim, holy and pleasing to God, and whose blood has become the instrument of atonement for the sins of all men. Justification is conferred in Baptism, the sacrament of faith. It conforms us to the righteousness of God, who makes us inwardly just by the power of his mercy. Its purpose is the glory of God and of Christ, and the gift of eternal life:

> But now the righteousness of God has been manifested apart from law, although the law and the prophets bear witness to it, the righteousness of God through faith in Jesus Christ for all who believe. For there is no distinction: since all have sinned and fall short of the glory of God, they are justified by his grace as a gift, through the redemption which is in Christ Jesus, whom God put forward as an expiation by his blood, to be received by faith. This was to show God's righteousness, because in his divine forbearance he had passed over former sins; it was to prove at the present time that he himself is righteous and that he justifies him who has faith in Jesus. [Rom. 3:21–26][19]

Who Really Bears the Burden?

Over the many months of study and prayer that preceded my return to Catholicism, I slowly began to understand why for so many years I did not, and many of my closest Protestants friends still do not, seem to *get* the Catholic view of justification. To understand what I mean, I want to conscript for my purposes an argument offered by a dear friend of mine who is a well-known Evangelical Protestant writer and speaker. He is a very bright man for whom I have tremendous respect. Like many Reformed writers, he sees the Christian believer's subjective certitude of an afterlife in heaven as the sine qua non of justification. He writes:

> I guess I would like to ask a Catholic, Do you know if you died at this moment whether you are going to heaven? Do you know that you have eternal life? When I was a Catholic myself I could never

say that. And even the Catholics that I talk to now think that it's kind of arrogant that you would know that you have eternal life, as if I know that I would merit it. I don't know I merit it, I know that Christ's merit applies to me and that's why I get it, so it wouldn't be arrogant from where I sit. But even that they would think that it was arrogant makes the point that it isn't all Christ that's doing this, in their view, that we're the ones who are meriting it and we will only know at the end of our lives. So the merit in this sense is keeping or adding to the score, as it were, and then we know after it's all over when we add up the points to see if we have a score that qualifies us for heaven. And if we do, we'd say that Christ did that through us.[20]

Setting aside the question of whether this is an accurate presentation of the Catholic view (and it should be clear by now that it is not), it seems that one can present the Reformed view in such a way that "works" are as much a necessary condition for justification as they are for the Catholic view. Remember, the Reformed view asserts that good works follow from true conversion and are part of one's post-justification sanctification. Presumably, if one claims to have been converted to Christ, i.e., justified, and no good works follow, then one was not ever really justified. This means that for the Protestant view of justification, *good works are a necessary condition for true justification.* The fact that the good works occur chronologically after conversion does not change their logical character as a necessary condition for justification. On the other hand, the Catholic view of justification requires a faith, wholly the work of God's grace, that involves more than mere intellectual assent, but is manifested in works of love, while being renewed and nurtured in prayer and the reception of the sacraments so that one may be conformed to the image of Christ. Thus, in a sense, both the Protestant and Catholic views require "works."

And neither view is better at establishing for the believer subjective certitude of heaven. For example, the Protestant, who said the sinner's prayer or answered an altar call, but shows no evidence of justification, is likely to have less certitude about his eternal fate than the faithful Catholic who, confident in God's promises, regularly attends Mass, receives the sacraments, engages in spiritual disciplines, and tries to obey the commands of Christ. This Catholic eagerly opens himself to the means of God's grace at his disposal. The Protestant can repeat the sinner's prayer and answer the altar call until the cows come home. But if she shows no evidence of justification, "good works," her eternal fate remains in serious doubt. On the other hand, one can no doubt find an obsessive-compulsive Catholic who quakes in his boots every day, wondering if he's done enough novenas or given enough alms to please God. Thus, what I am suggesting is that once one understands the Catholic view, though one may still wind up disagreeing with it, one should not dismiss it on irrelevant grounds, such as its apparent inability to provide absolute subjective assurance of heaven to its converts.

Because my friend begins with the Reformed belief that justification is forensic—that it is merely a matter of Christ's righteousness being imputed to us—he thinks that a Christian's cooperation with God's grace in the process of justification, as the Catholic understands it, is forensic as well. So, his error, it seems to me, rests in his understanding of grace, that it has no ontological status, that it is not a divine quality that can change nature over time in the soul of the believer who cooperates with God's free gift of grace. For my friend as well as many others, the "grace" the Christian acquires at his initial conversion (and/or baptism) is just the name the Bible attributes to the legal declaration that we are no longer considered guilty in the eyes of God for our sins because Christ took our punishment on the cross. Catholics, of course, do not deny that Christ died for all our sins or that he "offered his life to his Father through the Holy Spirit in reparation for our disobedience,"[21] or that "by one man's disobedience many were made sinners, so by one man's obedience many will be made righteous."[22] But, again, for Catholics the gift of grace is far more than a legal declaration. "It," in the words of the *Catechism*, "conforms us to the righteousness of God, who makes us inwardly just by the power of his mercy."[23]

The view that my friend holds, the Reformed doctrine of imputation, and its attendant understanding of grace, has its roots in a late medieval school of thought called *nominalism*, which comes from the Latin word for "name." According to this view, there are no natures or essences that living beings actually possess. The natures we ascribe to living beings are merely names (or "nominal essences") that are shorthand ways to label beings that have roughly similar characteristics. For this reason, nominalists were also voluntarists when it comes to God's moral law. Because God himself does not have a nature (for, they reasoned, to have a nature would limit God), then his moral law must be based exclusively on his will and not constrained by any intrinsically good nature. So, God could be capricious and arbitrary. Unfortunately, as many historical theologians have argued, nominalism shaped the thought of Luther and Calvin. This is why Reformed thinking fully embraces the forensic view of justification. As the English theologian E. L. Mascall explains:

> Now, by the end of the Middle Ages, nominalism was in the ascendant in philosophy and theology alike. . . . The consequence was that the reality of an object tended to be identified entirely with its observable characteristics. Each object was a separate bundle of sensible particulars; there were no real relations between beings, and in each individual being there was nothing but its observable behaviour. . . . How, then, is somebody whose whole mentality has been cast in the mould of nominalism to conceive the activity of justifying grace? He cannot think of it as consisting in a supernatural transformation of a man's being in its ontological depths *beneath* the observable level; for on nominalist principles there is nothing beneath the observable level to transform. On the other hand, if justifying grace were to consist of a transformation *on* the observable level, the man would be simply justified by his works; for on nominalistic principles a man's observable behaviour is neither more nor less than his total activity. What, then, was there left for Luther to say, being convinced, as he rightly was by St Paul, that a man cannot be justified by his works? Only this: that there is no real change in the man at all, but God treats him as if there was. By a sheer gratuitous act of his love God *imputes* to the man the merits of Christ; God treats him *as if* he were as sinless as Christ himself, while leaving him the sinner that he was.[24]

Given this framework, it is no wonder that my friend and other Reformed writers see the Catholic view as "Jesus plus works" and that the Bible teaches that justification is a type of divine deposit to which we must in faith assent in order to have our debt wiped clean, past, present, and future. But as I have tried to show, this account caricatures the Catholic view. Knowing my friend's intellectual integrity, I am confident that he did not intend to perpetuate a caricature. Rather, I believe that he was seeing the Catholic view through the lenses of forensic justification. But, the question that should have struck him as it has struck many of us, is this: why does one not find a full-blown doctrine of forensic justification prior to the Reformation era? One does not find it in the ante-Nicene, Nicene, or post-Nicene Fathers. One does not find it in the Latin or Eastern rites of the church. What does one find? One finds a view of grace and faith that is deeply biblical but conspicuously non-Reformed.

Because the Early Church was committed to the deep mystery of Chalcedonian Christology—Jesus of Nazareth was both fully God and fully man—it saw no need to divide faith and works, as if they were hostile foes. Thus, it saw a Christian's obedience, one's "works," as the exercise of faith by which the believer undergoes intrinsic transformation while in communion with God. For the Early Church, God became a human being so that human beings may become godly. After all, if works diminish faith's significance because our cooperation apparently limits God's sovereignty,[25] then why believe that Jesus really took on a human nature, for does not that imply that God was not sufficiently almighty enough to save us without acquiring a human nature?

According to the *Catechism of the Catholic Church*, "justification establishes *cooperation between God's grace and man's freedom*," and yet, "man's merit . . . itself is due to God."[26] So, the Christian, who by God's grace is given the power to cooperate with God's grace, cannot by her works earn the grace that she receives, just as the addition of a human nature contributed nothing to the divine status of the second person of the Trinity. Yet, in both cases, something wonderful has happened. To think that God's sovereignty is diminished by our cooperation is no different from thinking that Jesus was less divine because he took on a human nature.

112

The key to understanding Catholic theology is to set aside the assumption that it is always a zero-sum game. Justification is about our being part of a communion of saints, the body of Christ, with whom we can receive and share the unearned and totally gratuitous wonders of God's grace, through baptism, the Eucharist, confession, and all the sacraments. I do nothing without the initiation of the Holy Spirit. It is not my merit; it is his. And yet, there is a mystery here. I cooperate with this grace, but I contribute nothing to it. In my obedience, I am allowing the grace of God to transform me. And yet, it is wholly God's doing. I am confident of my eternal fate, but confidence in that eternal fate is not the exclusive purpose of justification. For God not only wants you to get to heaven, he wants to get heaven into you. And he does so by grace that has the power to change nature.

The great debates that divided the Church during its first 500 years were over the Trinitarian nature of God, the two natures of Jesus Christ, and Pelagianism. During this time, the canon of the New Testament was being fixed. And yet, the Church delivered to its people, without controversy as to their gracious efficacy and status as legitimate Christian practices, the sacraments of confession and the Eucharist, with the understanding that these practices imparted to the believer grace so that he or she may be made into the image of Christ. In the Eastern Church it is called deification (not because the believer could become a god, in the sense of acquiring the nature of the creator, but rather that the Christian life is a process of intrinsic change toward godliness that begins at Baptism and is totally the result of God's grace). So, a Reformed-type view of justification was not a point of controversy in the pre-Reformation era Church. After all, the only Church controversy that touched on the issue of justification—the Pelagian controversy—was resolved at the Council of Orange at which the Church offered a distinctly Catholic understanding of grace, faith, and justification. Thus, there is a heavy burden on the part of Reformed writers to show that the ascendancy in the sixteenth century of a Reformation thinking that had no ecclesiastical predecessors may be attributed to a return to the true understanding of Christianity.

The "Catholic" Practices

As I have noted, in addition to the Catholic doctrine of justification, three other issues had been barriers to my return to the Catholic Church: the Real Presence in the Eucharist, the teaching authority of the Church (including apostolic succession and the primacy of the Pope), and penance. As should be evident from the ancient Christian practices to which I alluded in my lengthy discussions on justification in both this chapter and the previous one, it did not take long for these other impediments to begin to dissolve as well.

I found that the Church Fathers affirmed, very early on, the Real Presence of Christ in the Eucharist,[27] infant baptism,[28] penance and confession,[29] an ordained priesthood,[30] and an episcopal ecclesiology and apostolic succession[31] (as well as other "Catholic" doctrines including prayers for the dead[32] and purgatory[33]). Even in the cases where these practices and doctrines were not articulated until their later, fuller formulations, their primitive versions were surely there. But this is also true of the doctrines of the Trinity and Incarnation as well as what constitutes the New Testament canon, all of which are embraced by Evangelical Protestants even though their mature articulations are not found in scripture.

But what was surprising to me is that one *never finds* in the Church Fathers' claims that these "Catholic" doctrines—for example, purgatory, apostolic succession, Real Presence in the Eucharist, infant baptism, penance—are "unbiblical," "heretical," "apostate," or "not Christian." So, at worst, I thought, the Catholic doctrines were considered legitimate options early on in church history. And this by the men who were discipled by the Apostles and/or the Apostles' disciples and/or their successors. At best, the Catholic doctrines are part of the deposit of faith passed on to the successors of the Apostles and preserved by the teaching authority of the Catholic Church.

I then purchased and read *Called to Communion* (1996) by Cardinal Joseph Ratzinger (Pope Benedict XVI) and *Rome Sweet Home* (1993), Scott and Kimberly Hahn's narrative of their journey to the Catholic Church. I also consulted the works of Catholic writers Jimmy Akin, Mark Brumley, and Carl Olson, which I discovered while surfing the internet. Like the Hahns, these three men are former Evangelical Protestants who know how to clearly communicate their Catholic faith to those with similar backgrounds.

After all that I had read and studied, this is what I concluded by mid-March 2007. It is his Apostles from which Jesus began his Church. From its infancy in the book of Acts, it was the Church that first testified to the Lordship of Christ and called people to follow him, which meant that one could, through repentance and baptism, become assimilated into that Body. Its earliest members produced the twenty-seven books we call the New Testament. Those books were promulgated and gradually recognized as scripture while the Church's theology and liturgy began to develop.[34] In fact, many of these books, including some that did not make the final New Testament canon that was fixed at the end of the fourth century, were an integral part of Christian worship that included their public recitation.[35] And it was in those local churches that the practices of confession and penance, belief in and celebration of the Real Presence of the Eucharist, prayers for and to the dead, and the idea of an ordained priesthood under the leadership of bishops, the Apostles' successors, took root, flourished, and developed throughout the Christian world. Thus, by mid-March 2007, I had come to accept the reasonableness of the Catholic understanding of ecclesiology and doctrine: that the Christian Church's theology and practices developed alongside, and in symbiotic relationship with, the production, formation, and selection of the New Testament canon. The conclusion appeared clear. Unless I capriciously cherry-picked the Catholic tradition, I could not justifiably accept the Early Church's recognition and fixation of the canon of scripture—and its correct determination and promulgation of the central doctrines of God and Christ (at Nicea and Chalcedon)—while rejecting the Church's sacramental life as well as its findings about its own apostolic nature and authority. I was boxed into a corner, with the only exit being a door to a confessional.

The Decision

At this point, I thought, if I reject the Catholic Church, there is good reason for me to believe I am rejecting the Church that Christ himself established. That's not a risk I was willing to take. (My wife did not need as much convincing. She had arrived at this destination some time earlier.) After all, if I return to the Church and participate in the Sacraments, I lose nothing, since I would still be a follower of Jesus and believe everything that the Catholic creeds teach, as I have always believed. But if the Church is right about itself and the Sacraments, I acquire graces I would have not otherwise received. Moreover, my parents had baptized me a Catholic, and made sure I was confirmed while I was in the seventh grade. For the first time, the commandment "Honor thy father and mother" carried with it an authority I had never entertained. It occurred to me that the burden was on me, and not on the Catholic Church, to show why I should remain in schism with the Church in which my parents baptized me, even as I could think of no incorrigible reason to remain in schism. So, on March 23, 2007, my wife and I met with a local priest, Fr. Timothy Vavarerk, and told him of our intent to seek full communion with the Church.

7

Evangelical and Catholic

Christian faith, understood in evangelical terms, is much more than an intellectual assent. It is a complex act involving the whole person—mind, will, and emotions. In believing I entrust myself to God as He makes Himself known by His word. Faith includes a cognitive element, for it could not arise unless one were intellectually convinced that God is, has spoken, and has said what we take to be His word. But in believing I entrust myself to this God and, if I am sincere, commit myself to live according to that word. An evangelically oriented theology will explore these various dimensions of faith.

Avery Cardinal Dulles, SJ (1996)[1]

Evangelicals, though historically hesitant to call themselves catholic because of what they see as incomplete Christianity among those, Roman and Anglican, who claim the name, are as catholic in purpose as anyone else, and their reluctance to use the label is a pity, just as it is a pity that self styled Anglican Catholics who love the Lord Jesus should hesitate to call themselves evangelicals. The essence of evangelicalism, as today's scholars usually define it, is bible-based, cross-centered, commitment-oriented (I forgo the word conversion here, since it begs questions), and mission-focused: four qualities that, one way or another have marked the Christian Church as such since it began (if you doubt me, look at St. Paul!). To suspect those who call themselves evangelicals of being standoffish within the church to the point of sectarianism, as has been done in times past, is unworthy and untrue.

J. I. Packer (2005)[2]

On May 5, 2007, I resigned as president of the Evangelical Theological Society (ETS) and two days latter I resigned my membership, one I held for over twenty years. I did so because I quickly realized after my conversion had become public that there was no way that ETS could conduct business with my continued presence on the executive committee or in its membership. In fact, soon after my resignations, two members proposed extensive changes to the organization's doctrinal statement. These changes, if passed, would leave no doubt that ETS excludes all non-Protestants from membership.[3] Thus, it seemed clear that if I did not resign my presidency and membership, my place in ETS would have been the focus of an intense debate within the society. Such a public and rancorous dispute over one individual would have needlessly ruptured many of my long-term friendships and alliances with members of ETS and the wider Evangelical world. And it may have also produced fissures in the growing collaboration and fellowship between Catholics and Protestants in the United States and abroad.

One may ask why I waited six days after my April 29, 2007 public reception into the Catholic Church to resign my ETS presidency and eight days to resign my membership. I did so because I did not believe that the ETS doctrinal statement was inconsistent with my Catholic beliefs. My resignations were motivated entirely by the reasons I stated in the previous paragraph. I did not want my return to the Catholic Church to cause needless offense to my brothers and sisters in Christ from whom I have learned so much in my over three decades in the Protestant world. Nevertheless, I still believe that the ETS doctrinal statement is broad enough to allow Catholic members. The purpose of this chapter is to explain why I believe this.

I know there are many friends and colleagues who will disagree with my reasoning and believe that ETS should remain exclusively Protestant. I understand and respect that point of view, and appreciate the sincere and thoughtful theological convictions that ground it. However, I believe that there is much to be gained from Catholic and Protestant scholars, committed to Christian orthodoxy and a high view of scripture, by interacting in an academic setting in which they may learn from each other.

The ETS Executive Committee Responds

Soon after my resignation my colleagues on the ETS executive committee issued a press release. It was a gracious and charitable statement that offered to its membership and the wider Christian world an argument as to why a Catholic could not be a member, let alone the president, of ETS. My friends on the committee were more than generous in their comments about my performance as 2006 program chair, as well as my academic work and its contribution to the church universal. I was deeply moved by this, and consider myself blessed to have served with men of such exceptional gifts and Christian charity.

However, I did not agree with their conclusions. But before I present and assess their press release, I need first to recount something of the history of ETS and the content of its doctrinal statement.[4]

The ETS was founded in 1949 "to foster conservative Biblical scholarship by providing a medium for the oral exchange and written expression of thought and research in the general field of the theological disciplines as centered in the scriptures." From its humble beginnings in Cincinnati in 1949, the ETS has grown to nearly 4500 members, over 2300 of whom now attend the annual meeting. Among these members are many of the leading conservative Protestant scholars in the United States and Canada. Also included are overseas missionaries and students engaged in graduate work. Most members are professors from a wide variety of disciplines such as theology, biblical studies, philosophy, history, religion, and intercultural studies. Members represent virtually every Protestant denomination as well as both secular and religious institutions. There are, to my knowledge, some Anglo-Catholic and Eastern Orthodox members, though they keep a low profile. The ETS publishes a scholarly periodical, the *Journal of the Evangelical Theological Society*, which was launched in 1958. With all the work and activity of this vibrant society, it has only a single, two-sentence doctrinal requirement for membership. One must affirm:

> The Bible alone, and the Bible in its entirety, is the Word of God written and is therefore inerrant in the autographs. God is a Trinity, Father, Son, and Holy Spirit, each an uncreated person, one in essence, equal in power and glory.

In its press release after my resignation, the ETS executive committee explained why it believes that a devout Catholic cannot, in principle, agree to this doctrinal statement:

> The work of the Evangelical Theological Society as a scholarly forum proceeds on the basis that "the Bible alone, and the Bible in its entirety, is the Word of God written and is therefore inerrant in the autographs." This affirmation, together with the statement on the Trinity, forms the basis for membership in the ETS to which all members annually subscribe in writing. Confessional Catholicism, as defined by the Roman Catholic Church's declarations from the Council of Trent to Vatican II, sets forth a more expansive view of verbal, infallible revelation.
>
> Specifically, it posits a larger canon of Scripture than that recognized by evangelical Protestants, including in its canon several writings from the Apocrypha. It also extends the quality of infallibility to certain expressions of church dogma issued by the Magisterium (the teaching office of the Roman Catholic Church), as well as certain pronouncements of the pope, which are delivered ex cathedra, such as doctrines about the immaculate conception and assumption of Mary.
>
> We recognize the right of Roman Catholic theologians to do their theological work on the basis of all the authorities they consider to be revelatory and infallible, even as we wholeheartedly affirm

the distinctive contribution and convictional necessity of the work of the Evangelical Theological Society on the basis of the "Bible alone and the Bible in its entirety" as "the Word of God written and . . . inerrant."

I will now explain why I do not agree with my esteemed colleagues' understanding of the ETS doctrinal statement, or their depiction of the Catholic doctrine of scripture and its relationship to the Church and its authority.

A Response to the Executive Committee

The ETS doctrinal statement asserts more than just a view of scripture. It also makes a claim about the nature of the Deity, that "God is a Trinity, Father, Son, and Holy Spirit, each an uncreated person, one in essence, equal in power and glory." But this claim and all the rich metaphysical ideas it imports without attribution from the victorious side of the intra-Christian debates of the fourth century that resulted in the Nicene Creed—"person," "one in essence," "equal in power and glory"—are not explicitly stated in the inerrant Bible that the ETS maintains is alone the Word of God. Assuming that the ETS believes that its formulation of the doctrine of the Trinity is a true description of God, then this formulation is an item of revelation, theological knowledge that one could not have arrived at without God's having chosen to reveal it. For this formulation is not a deliverance of natural theology, something that one could discover with unaided natural reason. But this would mean that ETS accepts "a more expansive view of verbal, infallible revelation," which puts ETS in precisely the same position it attributes to the Catholic Church.

Suppose, however, the ETS denies that its formulation of the Trinity is theological knowledge, asserting that it is merely the organization's belief—take it or leave it. But that doesn't seem right, since the first half of the doctrinal statement (the ETS view of scripture) is claimed by its proponents as a true description of the nature of the Bible. Its proponents do not merely maintain that this belief is "their tradition," which they believe those outside of that tradition are not required to embrace. Rather, they actually believe their doctrine of scripture is true and that others ought to believe it as well. So, it seems fair to say that the Trinity formulation is on par with the ETS view of scripture.

The ETS executive committee points out in its letter that the Catholic Bible has in its Old Testament canon seven books (called "deutero-canonical" by Catholics and "the apocrypha" by Protestants) that are not in the Protestant Old Testament. That is certainly true, but it's not clear why that is a sufficient reason to exclude Catholics from ETS (or exclude Eastern Orthodox believers, at least one of whom is presently an ETS member).

First, although no one doubts that the founders of ETS had the Protestant canon in mind when they used the word "Bible," they were sophisticated enough to know that most Christians in the world, both East and West, belong to communions that accept the Catholic canon, which is the canon recognized by the local councils of Hippo (AD 393) and Carthage III (AD 397).[5] Although some individuals in the Church raised questions about whether the deutero-canonical books should be included in the biblical canon, no synod, council, or body within Western or Eastern Christendom explicitly rejected these books as non-canonical prior to the Reformers doing so in the sixteenth century.

By not defining the scope of the canon or employing it as a specific criterion of membership, were the ETS founders purposely leaving the door slightly ajar for non-Protestants to join? We can only speculate, since only one living founder, Roger Nicole, has addressed this subject, claiming that the inerrancy statement was intended to exclude Catholics.[6] That may be true, but without hearing from the other founders, we really don't know. (It would be like interpreting the U.S. Constitution by relying exclusively on Alexander Hamilton's thoughts about it.) Moreover, the instrument used for the exclusion—the inerrancy statement—was clearly inadequate for the task, as Ray Van Neste persuasively argues.[7] If Professor Nicole, for example, had claimed that the screen door he attached to his home was intended to stop a flood, we would begin to wonder if he really knew the meaning of the word "flood." Thus, Professor Nicole's "intent," though relevant, is not sufficient if he did not truly understand what he was trying to stop. Because the Catholicism that Professor Nicole had in mind was not the Catholicism that is actually embraced by the Catholic Church; his intent, ironically, should permit, rather than forbid, Catholics from becoming members of ETS.

Second, at the 2006 meeting, while I was serving as President-Elect, the membership passed a resolution that added this statement to the bylaws: "For the purpose of advising members regarding the intent and meaning of the reference to biblical inerrancy in the ETS Doctrinal Basis, the Society refers members to the *Chicago Statement on Biblical Inerrancy* (1978)."[8] But the *Chicago Statement on Biblical Inerrancy* not only does not provide a list of canonical books, it states that "it appears that the Old Testament canon had been fixed by the time of Jesus. The New Testament canon is likewise now closed, inasmuch as no new apostolic witness to the historical Christ can now be borne."[9] But this, ironically, means that the ETS is implicitly showing sympathies for the *Catholic canon!* For, as J. N. D. Kelly points out,

> It should be observed that the Old Testament thus admitted as authoritative by the Church was somewhat bulkier and more comprehensive than . . . the Hebrew Bible of Palestinian Judaism . . . It always included, though with varying degrees of recognition, the so-called Apocryphal or deutero-canonical books. The reason for this is that the Old Testament which passed in the first instance into the hands of Christians was not the original Hebrew version, but the Greek translation known as the Septuagint. . . . In the first centuries at any rate the Church seems to have accepted all, or most of, these additional books as inspired and treated them without question as Scripture.[10]

Third, because the list of canonical books is itself not found in scripture—as one can find the Ten Commandments or the names of Christ's Apostles—any such list, whether Protestant or Catholic, would be an item of extra-biblical theological knowledge.[11] Take for example a portion of the revised and expanded ETS statement of faith suggested by the two ETS members following my return to the Catholic Church. It states that "this written word of God consists of the 66 books of the Old and New Testaments and is the supreme authority in all matters of belief and behavior."[12] But the belief that the Bible consists only of 66 books is not a claim *of* scripture—since one cannot find the list in it—but a claim *about* scripture as a whole. That is, the whole has a property—"consisting of 66 books"—that is not found in any of the parts. In other words, if the 66 books are the supreme authority on matters of belief, and the number of books is a belief, and one cannot find that belief in any of the books, then the belief that scripture consists of 66 particular books is an extra-biblical belief.[13] This would by implication now bring another item of revelation into the ETS orbit of inerrant beliefs that already includes the Trinity statement and the original inerrancy statement about scripture.

Thus, if the list of canonical books and the ETS statement as a whole (the statement on scripture and the statement on the Trinity) are themselves items of inerrant theological knowledge—which the ETS must accept in order to ward off the charge of incoherency—then, again, the ETS accepts "a more expansive view of verbal, infallible revelation" than the ETS claims to accept. For this means that the ETS, according to the executive committee's letter, requires that its members accept at least three truths as items of theological knowledge, the first two of which are clearly extra-biblical: (1) the list of canonical books, (2) its formulation of the doctrine of the Trinity, and (3) the statement on biblical inerrancy.

In the Second Vatican Council's 1965 Dogmatic Constitution on Divine Revelation, *Dei Verbum*, the Catholic Church affirms, just as the ETS affirms, that the Bible is God's inerrant word written:

> Therefore, since everything asserted by the inspired authors or sacred writers must be held to be asserted by the Holy Spirit, it follows that the books of Scripture must be acknowledged as teaching solidly, faithfully and without error that truth which God wanted put into sacred writings for the sake of salvation. Therefore "all Scripture is divinely inspired and has its use for teaching the truth and refuting error, for reformation of manners and discipline in right living, so that the man who belongs to God may be efficient and equipped for good work of every kind" (2 Tim. 3:16–17, Greek text).[14]

The inerrancy of scripture was also affirmed in 1870 by the First Vatican Council:

> These books [of the Old and New Testaments] the Church holds to be sacred and canonical not because she subsequently approved them by her authority after they had been composed by unaided human skill, nor simply because they contain revelation without error, but because, being written under the inspiration of the Holy Spirit, they have God as their author, and were as such committed to the Church.[15]

Moreover, the Catholic Church does not hold, contrary to what the ETS press release claims, that the infallibility of the Magisterium and the ex cathedra papal pronouncements are of the same nature as the Word of God written. As *Dei Verbum* states (as translated in the *Catechism of the Catholic Church*): "Yet *this Magisterium is not superior to the Word of God, but is its servant.* It teaches only what has been handed on to it. At the divine command and with the help of the Holy Spirit, it listens to this devotedly, guards it with dedication and expounds it faithfully. All that it proposes for belief as being divinely revealed is drawn from this single deposit of faith" (emphasis added).[16]

According to the Church, the Bible itself, though infallible, arose from the life of the Church, in its liturgical practices and theological reflections. It is a source of theological truth, to be sure, and uniquely the Word of God written. But the Church maintains, quite sensibly, that the Bible cannot be read in isolation from the historic Church and the practices that were developing alongside the Church's creeds—creeds that became permanent benchmarks of orthodoxy during the same eras in which the canon of scripture itself was finally fixed.[17] So, for the Catholic, the Magesterium and the Papacy are limited by both scripture and a particular understanding of Christian doctrine, forged by centuries of debate and reflection, and, in many cases, fixed by ecumenical councils. Consequently, the Catholic Church and its leadership are far more constrained from doctrinal innovation than either the ETS or the typical Evangelical megachurch pastor.

For example, Gregory Boyd, a Baptist theologian and pastor of a Minneapolis congregation, denies that God knows the future, and bases this denial on a literal reading of scripture. This is called the Open View of God, or Open Theism. Two of Boyd's fellow open theists, Clark Pinnock and John P. Sanders, could not be removed as members of ETS in a 2003 membership-wide vote initiated by Professor Nicole. (For the record, I voted *against* removing these men from ETS because I do not believe its doctrinal statement is inconsistent with open theism, even though I think that open theism is deeply flawed.) Sanders and Pinnock affirm both inerrancy and the Trinity, and they seem to embrace these views sincerely and without mental reservation. Yet, in contrast to Pastor Boyd, Pope Benedict XVI has far less power to steer his Church's doctrine in any direction he may find consistent with his own professional theological project. For the Pope is constrained by settled doctrine—including scripture, ecumenical councils, and prior ex cathedra papal pronouncements. Pastors and theologians like Boyd, Pinnock, and Sanders are constrained only by "inerrancy" and "the Trinity," which means (at least theoretically) that they could embrace any one of a variety of heresies condemned by the ancient Church and yet still remain an ETS member in good standing: Nestorianism,[18] Monophysitism,[19] Pelagianism,[20] semi-Pelagianism,[21] or the denial of Christ's eternal sonship.[22] Yet oddly, Catholics who embrace the Church that claimed to have the ecclesiastical authority to condemn these heresies, and which provided to its separated progeny, including Evangelicals, the resources and creeds that provide the grounds for excluding these heresies, apparently have no place in ETS. What's more, Augustine, whose genius helped rid the Church of the Pelagian and semi-Pelagian heresies,[23] would not be welcomed in ETS or as a faculty member at virtually any evangelical seminary, because the Bishop of Hippo accepted the deutero-canonical books as part of the Old Testament canon,[24] the deposit of sacred tradition,[25] apostolic succession,[26] the gracious efficacy of the sacraments,[27] the Real Presence of the Eucharist,[28] baptismal regeneration,[29] and the infusion of God's grace for justification.[30]

Evangelical and Catholic

After all the theoretical wrangling is over, one should ask a deeply practical question: what would be lost if the Evangelical Theological Society were to include Catholics who embrace a high view of scripture? Perhaps we would learn from our Protestant friends and they would learn from us. Is that so objectionable? My sense is that this cross-pollination cannot help but enrich each other's perspectives. I know one counterargument is, "That's what the American Academy of Religion (AAR) and Society of Biblical Literature (SBL) are for!" But I think that response misses a deeper point: serious Catholics and Protestants share much more with each other than they do with a wide range of religious traditions and philosophical perspectives that are represented at AAR and SBL. We share a commitment to Christian orthodoxy and a high view of scripture, something that one is unlikely to find at the AAR among participants who deliver papers with titles like "S/M Rituals in Gay Men's Leather Communities: Initiation, Power Exchange, and Subversion" and "In Church There Is No Beer: Polka Mass as a Regional Devotion."[31]

As post-Vatican II Catholicism has become more attentive to scripture, precisely because of its willingness to take Protestantism more seriously than in the past, early twenty-first century Evangelical Protestantism has become more aware of the debt it owes to the Catholic and Orthodox traditions in which and from which creedal Christianity developed alongside of and in relationship with the formation of the canon of scripture. Evangelical Protestantism's increasing appreciation of these traditions is most evident in the growing scholarship in patristic studies and medieval Christian philosophy, the expanding interest in the spiritual disciplines and contemplative prayer by thinkers like Dallas Willard and J. P. Moreland, and the rising though selective incorporation of high church liturgical practices in the Emergent Church movement as well as by some low church Protestant congregations.

Thus, it is surely true that contemporary Evangelicalism has its roots in conservative Protestantism, but it is no less true that Protestantism itself has its roots in *Catholicism*. So if it's a matter of theological and ecclesiastical patrimony, one could just as easily say that Evangelical Protestantism is another distant cousin in the Catholic family. Moreover, contemporary Evangelicalism has been shaped by the Catholic and Protestant charismatic and Pentecostal movements as well as the spirituality and apologetics of authors like C. S. Lewis, who, though an Anglican, produced works that are "Catholic" in their tone and substance. This is why Lewis is one of the most beloved writers among Catholics as well as Evangelical Protestants. Consequently, if one thinks of Evangelicalism as a renewal movement that stresses personal conversion and spiritual development, evangelism, a high view of scripture, and fidelity to Christian orthodoxy, then one can certainly be an Evangelical Catholic.

Put in terms of specific traditions, if the term "Evangelical" is broad enough to include high-church Anglicans, low-church anti-creedal Baptists, Presbyterians, Methodists, the Evangelical Free Church, Arminians, Calvinists, Disciples of Christ, Pentecostals, Seventh-Day Adventists, open theists, atemporal theists, social Trinitarians, substantial Trinitarians, nominalists, realists, eternal security supporters and opponents, temporal theists, dispensationalists, theonomists, church-state separationists, church-state accomodationists, cessationists, non-cessationists, kenotic theorists, covenant theologians, paedo-Baptists, Anabaptists, and Dooyeweerdians, then there should be room for an Evangelical Catholic.

Pressing On

At the end of the day, I am an Evangelical Catholic because I believe in the *Evangel*, the Gospel, the Good News, and that it is a gift of God that ought to be embraced and lived by everyone. As an Evangelical, indeed as a Christian, I have an obligation to spread the Good News of Jesus Christ. I am Catholic insofar as I believe that the Church is universal and that its continuity is maintained through history by the whole of its membership, the Body of Christ, and not *merely* as a collection of isolated individuals in personal relationship with Jesus. I also believe that this Catholic Church is under the direction of the Holy Spirit working through the Church's Magisterium, the Apostles' successors.

Nevertheless, I also believe, as the *Catechism of the Catholic Church* teaches, that "'many elements of sanctification and of truth' are found outside the visible confines of the Catholic Church: 'the written Word of God; the life of grace; faith, hope, and charity, with the other interior gifts of the Holy Spirit, as well as visible elements.'"[32] "Christ's Spirit," the *Catechism* instructs us, "uses these Churches and ecclesial communities as means of salvation, whose power derives from the fullness of grace and truth that Christ has entrusted to the Catholic Church. All these blessings come from Christ and lead to him, and are in themselves calls to 'Catholic unity.'"[33] For this reason I am convinced that if not for the Holy Spirit working through the many gifted and devoted Christian scholars and teachers in Evangelical Protestantism, some of whom I have had the privilege to know, love, and study under, my present faith would be significantly diminished. Their tenacious defense and practice of Christian orthodoxy is what has sustained and nourished so many of us who have found our way back to the Church of our youth.

Although it may be difficult to detect from much of what I have written in this book, my return to the Catholic Church had as much to do with a yearning for a deeper spiritual life as it did with theological reasoning. Since becoming Catholic, I have become much more prayerful, I read the Bible far more often, and I am increasingly more aware and appreciative of the grace God has given me to live a virtuous life. I sometimes find myself silently praying a "Hail Mary" or an "Our Father" while driving or working out. I am not averse to asking particular saints to pray for me, or to recite the prayers of some of my favorite saints, such as Thomas Aquinas. When doing this I gain a greater sense of that of which I am a part, the wonderful Body of Christ that transcends time, space, and death itself. Since becoming Catholic I have participated in such practices as praying the rosary and praying the Stations of the Cross. These practices are rich and good, but the sacrament of reconciliation (or confession) has been the most liberating aspect of my Catholic experience so far. Although many Catholics acquire a deeper walk with God through the Real Presence of Christ in the Eucharist, I have found confession to be the place in which I experience the gratuitous charity of our Lord at its fullest.

There can be no better way for me to conclude this book than to employ the words of that great nineteenth-century convert from Anglicanism to Catholicism, John Henry Cardinal Newman. Although he is writing of his own journey, Cardinal Newman seems to capture my present sense of things, my understanding of myself as both Evangelical and Catholic:

> From the time that I became a Catholic, of course I have no further history of my religious opinions to narrate. In saying this, I do not mean to say that my mind has been idle, or that I have given up thinking on theological subjects; but that I have had no changes to record, and have had no anxiety of heart whatever. I have been in perfect peace and contentment. I never have had one doubt. I was not conscious to myself, on my conversion, of any difference of thought or of temper from what I had before. I was not conscious of firmer faith in the fundamental truths of revelation, or of more self-command; I had not more fervour; but it was like coming into port after a rough sea; and my happiness on that score remains to this day without interruption.[34]

Soli Deo Gloria.

Notes

Introduction

1. G. K. Chesterton, *The Autobiography of G. K. Chesterton* (San Francisco: Ignatius Press, 2006; the original 1936 American edition was republished in this volume), 87.

2. I am borrowing this illustration from comments made by Paul J. Griffiths (Duke Divinity School) at a panel discussion of the Intra-Christian Conversion Study Group in which we participated at the 2007 meeting of the American Academy Religion in San Diego, California (November 16, 2007).

3. Included among Evangelical Protestants who are former Catholics are mega-church pastor Rick Warren (Saddleback Church), popular apologist Gregory P. Koukl (Stand to Reason), biblical scholar Thomas R. Schreiner (The Southern Baptist Theological Seminary), and theologian David Gushee (Mercer University). There are many others, some of whom are prominent pastors, speakers, scholars, and writers, virtually all of whom, like me, left Catholicism early in their lives.

4. Among those who have taken this trek are the Rt. Rev. Jeffrey N. Steenson (former Episcopalian Bishop of the Rio Grande), theologian Scott Hahn (Franciscan University, Steubenville), former Lutheran pastor Richard John Neuhaus (*First Things*), theologian R. R. Reno (Creighton University), and philosophers Robert C. Koons (University of Texas, Austin), J Budziszewski (University of Texas, Austin), Alasdair MacIntyre (University of Notre Dame), and Paul J. Griffiths (Duke University).

5. St. Augustine, Sermon 43, 7, 9: PL 38, 257–58.

6. C. S. Lewis, *The Weight of Glory and Other Addresses* (New York: Macmillan, 1949), 50.

Chapter 1 Confession on the Brazos

1. St. Augustine, *The Confessions of St. Augustine*, ed. Michael P. Foley, trans. F. J. Seed (Indianapolis: Hackett Publishing, 2006), 3.

2. "Academia," *World Magazine* 21, no. 38 (October 7, 2006).

3. Francis J. Beckwith, J. P. Moreland, and William Lane Craig, eds., *To Everyone An Answer* (Downers Grove, IL: InterVarsity Press, 2004).

4. Beckwith, "Introduction," in ibid., 14–15.

Chapter 2 Viva Las Vegas

1. Frank Marino, "The Game of H.O.R.S.E.: Top 10 – Bottom 10" (June 2007), available at http://www.vegascommunityonline.com/2007/06/WSOP-w3.htm (March 9, 2008).

2. So much so that over 25 years later I actually published a philosophical essay assessing Dylan's Christian work: Francis J. Beckwith, "Busy Being Born Again: Bob Dylan's Christian Philosophy," in *Bob Dylan and Philosophy: It's Alright, Ma (I'm Only Thinking)*, ed. Peter Vernezze and Carl Porter (Chicago: Open Court Publishing, 2006), 145–55.

3. According to my wife, I am still given to emotional outbursts. (Disclaimer: She made me write this.)

4. There are many things I did not know then that I believe helps account for the vibrancy I encountered and still encounter among Evangelical Protestants. For instance, the French Lutheran convert to Catholicism, Louis Bouyer, correctly attributes these spiritual virtues to Protestantism's recovery of, and reliance on, aspects of the Catholic tradition. See Louis Bouyer, *The Spirit and Forms of Protestantism* (London: The Harvill Press, 1956).

5. Unfortunately, my intuitions turned out to be right. Years later I found out that the commune had quickly morphed into an authoritarian regime that required from its members near absolute obedience to the leadership on virtually every important question in one's life. In short, it became a cult.

6. For my Catholics readers, this occurs often among Evangelical Protestants. It is sometimes called "rededicating your life to the Lord." In a weird way it is the Protestant version of the sacrament of reconciliation. It's almost as if by nature we human beings need something like that, and for that reason Evangelical Protestants have developed a practice that Catholics have practiced more formally for centuries.

7. See, for example, Mitch Pacwa, SJ, "Tell Me Who I Am, O Enneagram," *Christian Research Journal* 14, no. 2 (Fall 1991): 14–19.

8. See, for example, Francis J. Beckwith, Carl Mosser, and Paul Owen, eds., *The New Mormon Challenge: Responding to the Latest Defenses of a Fast-Growing Movement* (Grand Rapids: Zondervan; New York: HarperCollins, 2002); Francis J. Beckwith and Stephen E. Parrish, *The Mormon Concept of God: A Philosophical Analysis,* Studies in American Religion, volume 55 (Lewiston, NY: Edwin Mellen Press, 1991); Francis J. Beckwith, "Sects in the City: Mormonism and the Philosophical Perils of Being a Missionary Faith," *The Southern Baptist Journal of Theology* 9, no. 2 (Summer 2005): 14–30; and Francis J. Beckwith, "Mormon Theism, the Traditional Christian Concept of God, and Greek Philosophy: A Critical Analysis." *Journal of the Evangelical Theological Society* 44, no. 4 (December 2001): 671–95.

9. See, for example, the hugely successful book by Ed Decker and Dave Hunt, *The God Makers: A Shocking Exposé of What the Mormon Church Really Believes*, updated and expanded edition (Eugene, OR: Harvest House, 1997). In 1998 I made the mistake of contributing a chapter to a book called *The Counterfeit Gospel of Mormonism*

(Harvest House, 1997). Although I stand by the content of my chapter, which dealt with the nature of God in Mormonism and classical Christian theism, the book's title and cover (which featured models posing as a very white looking LDS family), as well as the way the publisher marketed the work, were an embarrassment to me. They were inconsistent with the way I had chosen to conduct myself as a Christian academic. Thankfully, the book is now out of print. And given its publisher's penchant to distribute hysterically bad anti-Catholic tomes, I doubt that my now-Catholic contribution would be welcomed if a reprint or revised edition were in the offing.

Chapter 3 Summa Apologia

1. *Summa Theologiae* 2–2, ques. 188, art. 6, as quoted in Alfred J. Fredosso, "*Fides et Ratio*: A 'Radical' Vision of Intellectual Inquiry," available at http://www.nd.edu/~afreddos/papers/f&r-radicalvision.htm#N_16_ (May 22, 2008).

2. J. P. Moreland, "Philosophical Apologetics, the Church, and Contemporary Culture," *Journal of the Evangelical Theological Society* 39, no. 1 (March 1996): 130.

3. In contrast, my 2005 chapter on Baha'ism in Ronald Enroth's *Guide to New Religious Movements* offers just the sort of tone and quality of argument that my twenty-four-year-old self could not possibly have possessed. See Francis J. Beckwith, "The Baha'i World Faith," in *Guide to New Religious Movements*, ed. Ronald Enroth, 2nd ed. (Downers Grove, IL: InterVarsity Press, 2005), 155–68, 207–11.

4. Francis J. Beckwith and Michael E. Bauman, eds., *Are You Politically Correct? Debating America's Cultural Standards* (Amherst, NY: Prometheus Books, 1993); Michael E. Bauman and Francis J. Beckwith, eds., *A Summit Reader: Essays and Lectures in Honor of David Noebel's 70th Birthday* (Manitou Springs, CO: Summit Press, 2007).

5. (AD 325) First Council of Nicaea; (AD 381) First Council of Constantinople; (AD 431) Council of Ephesus; (AD 451) Council of Chalcedon; (AD 553) Second Council of Constantinople; (AD 680) Third Council of Constantinople.

6. For example, the Orthodox Presbyterian Church states on its website: "For several centuries the church struggled to clarify its understanding of the Bible in opposition to error. The church formulated basic doctrines about God and Christ in such creeds as the Apostles' Creed and the Nicene Creed. We share these great ecumenical creeds with other Christians" ("What is the Orthodox Presbyterian Church? Basic Information to Acquaint You with the Orthodox Presbyterian Church," available at http://www.opc.org/whatis.html [March 30, 2008]).

Chapter 4 No Direction Home

1. Herman Melville, *White-Jacket or the World in a Man-of-War* (Boston: The Botolph Society, 1892), 374.

2. Ryan T. Anderson, "For Humanity," *National Review* (October 8, 2007): 68–70 (review of *Defending Life: A Moral and Legal Case Against Abortion Choice* by Francis J. Beckwith); M. D. Aesliman, "Providence Lost—and Found?" *National Review* (September 9, 2003): 46–48 (review of *Law, Darwinism, and Public Education: The Establishment Clause and the Challenge of Intelligent Design* by Francis J. Beckwith); Brad Stetson, a review of *Politically Correct Death: Answering the Arguments for Abortion Rights* by Francis J. Beckwith, *National Review* (October 10, 1994): 81.

3. Here is the relevant excerpt from that homily:

Having a clear faith, based on the Creed of the Church, is often labeled today as a fundamentalism. Whereas, relativism, which is letting oneself be tossed and "swept along by every wind of teaching," looks like the only attitude (acceptable) to today's standards. We are moving towards a dictatorship of relativism which does not recognize anything as for certain and which has as its highest goal one's own ego and one's own desires.

"Homily of His Eminence Card. Joseph Ratzinger, Dean of the College of Cardinals" (April 18, 2005), available at http://www.vatican.va/gpII/documents/homily-pro eligendo-pontifice_20050418_en.html (April 11, 2008).

4. Peer review column, *The Chronicle of Higher Education* 53, no. 3 (September 8, 2006): A5.

5. *Catechism of the Catholic Church: Revised in Accordance With the Official Latin Text Promulgated by Pope John Paul II*, 2nd ed. (Washington, DC: United States Conference of Catholic Bishops, 2000), 1260.

Chapter 5 Wisdom of My Ancestors

1. William F. Buckley Jr., *Up From Liberalism* (New York: Hillman, 1961), 219.

2. John Henry Cardinal Newman, *An Essay on the Development of Christian Doctrine*, 6th ed. (Notre Dame, IN: University of Notre Dame Press, 1989; reprint of 1878 edition), 7, 8.

3. See Louis Bouyer, *The Spirit and Forms of Protestantism* (London: The Harvill Press, 1956).

4. Joseph Cardinal Ratzinger, *Truth and Tolerance: Christian Belief and World Religions*, ed. Henry Taylor (San Francisco: Ignatius Press, 2004), 184.

5. *The Westminster Confession of Faith* (1646), chapter I, sec. VI, available at http://www.reformed.org/documents/wcf_with_proofs/ (April 19, 2008).

6. D. H. Williams, *Evangelicals and Tradition: The Formative Influence of the Early Church* (Grand Rapids: Baker Academic, 2005), 97.

7. Oliver Wendell Holmes, "The Path of the Law," *Harvard Law Review* 10 (1897).

8. Bertrand Russell, *Introduction to Mathematical Philosophy* (London: Routledge, 1919; reprinted 1993), 71. Nevertheless, I am still convinced that the *sola scriptura* of the Magisterial Reformers is really the only coherent Protestant view that has the theological resources to ward off the ahistorical individualism of the isolated Christian whose "Bible" becomes a reservoir of proof-texts for one's dogmatic proclivities (or what Keith Mathison calls *solo scriptura*). See Mathison's thoughtful tome, *The Shape of Sola Scriptura* (Moscow, ID: Canon, 2001), 346–47.

9. For example, consider the verses in 2 Timothy that are often employed as part of a biblical case for *sola scriptura*: "All Scripture is God-breathed and is useful for teaching, rebuking, correcting and training in righteousness, so that all God's people may be thoroughly equipped for every good work" (2 Tim. 3:16–17 TNIV). No doubt, if *sola scriptura* is true, this isolated passage would at best lend support for it or at worst not be inconsistent with it. But it certainly does not establish it. For this reason, it is difficult to see how one can get the Reformation doctrine of *sola scriptura* out of

this passage. (See Craig A. Allert, *A High View of Scripture?: The Authority of the Bible and the Formation of the New Testament* [Grand Rapids: Baker Academic, 2007], 150–52.)

The wider context of this passage is also problematic for a Reformed understanding of *sola scriptura*. In verse 13 Paul contrasts Timothy with "evildoers and impostors" and then in verses 14 and 15 pleads with him to "continue in what you have learned and have become convinced of, because you know those from whom you learned it, and how from infancy you have known the Holy Scriptures, which are able to make you wise for salvation through faith in Christ Jesus." Paul then makes a general claim about scripture as "God-breathed," as well as being "useful for teaching, rebuking, correcting and training in righteousness, so that all God's people may be thoroughly equipped for every good work" (2 Tim. 3:16–17). What stands out is that Paul's instructions include appeals to tradition: his own teachings as well as what Timothy has learned because he "know[s] those from whom he [learned it]." These instructions are so that Timothy may live a life of holiness ("training in righteousness"), fidelity to the Christian faith ("continue in what you have learned and have become convinced of"), and good works. To be sure, scripture is useful in equipping Timothy, but it *is not isolated from the Church and the traditions that contributed to Timothy's spiritual development.* Thus, it is difficult to see how one can get the Reformation doctrine of *sola scriptura* out of 2 Tim. 3:16–17 when its wider context is taken into account.

10. Because there can be no scriptural test for canonicity unless one first knows what constitutes scripture, one must rely on extra-scriptural tests in order to know the *scriptura* to which *sola scriptura* refers. But then one is not actually relying on "scripture alone" to determine the most fundamental standard for the Christian, the Bible. This means that *sola scriptura* is a first-order principle whose content must be determined by one or more second-order extra-scriptural principle.

11. This is a bit dicey, since it was only local, and not ecumenical, councils that provided an official list of canonical books in the end of the fourth and the beginning of the fifth centuries. Kelly notes that the canon was recognized by the local councils of Hippo (AD 393) and Carthage III (AD 397) as well as "in the famous letter which Pope Innocent I dispatched to Exuperius, bishop of Toulouse, in 405" (J. N. D. Kelly, *Early Christian Doctrines*, rev. ed. [San Francisco: HarperOne, 1978], 56).

12. John Henry Cardinal Newman, *Discussions and Arguments on Various Subjects* (New York: Longmans, Green, and Co., 1907), 144–45.

13. *Catechism of the Catholic Church: Revised in Accordance With the Official Latin Text Promulgated by Pope John Paul II*, 2nd ed. (Washington, DC: United States Conference of Catholic Bishops, 2000).

14. The Church Fathers are traditionally divided into two categories in temporal relation to the dissemination of the Nicene Creed in AD 325: the Ante-Nicene Fathers, prior to AD 325; the Nicene and Post-Nicene Fathers, AD 325–787, the year of the Second Council of Nicaea.

15. See Avery Cardinal Dulles, "Justification: The Joint Declaration," *Josephinum Journal of Theology* 9, no. 1 (Winter/Spring 2002): 108–19.

16. Carl R. Trueman, review of *Is the Reformation Over?* by Mark A. Noll and Carolyn Nystrom, *Reformation21: The Online Magazine of the Alliance of Confessing Evangelicals* (November 2005), available at http://www.reformation21.org/Shelf_life/is-the-reformation-over.php (April 19, 2008).

17. Norman L. Geisler and Ralph MacKenzie, *Roman Catholics and Evangelicals: Agreements and Differences* (Grand Rapids: Baker Books, 1995), 103.

18. Alister McGrath, *Iustitia Dei: A History of the Christian Doctrine of Justification*, 3rd ed. (New York: Cambridge University Press, 2005), 217.

19. It should be noted that Luther seemed to believe that a Christian may fall from grace and "lose salvation." How this squares with a forensic view of justification is unclear. This is why I believe that Calvin's approach is more coherent. See, for example, Luther's commentary on the fifth chapter of Galatians in Martin Luther, *Commentary on the Epistle to the Galatians*, trans. Theodore Graebner (Grand Rapids: Zondervan,1949; originally published in 1535), 194–216.

20. Shortly after writing this I discovered that Peter J. Kreeft wrote something similar: "We do not do good works to get to heaven, but we do good works because heaven has gotten to us" (Peter J. Kreeft, *Catholic Christianity: A Complete Catechism of Catholic Beliefs Based on the* Catechism of the Catholic Church [San Francisco: Ignatius Press, 2001], 126).

21. The *Catechism* states:

> The grace of the Holy Spirit has the power to justify us, that is, to cleanse us from our sins and to communicate to us "the righteousness of God through faith in Jesus Christ" and through Baptism. . . .
>
> Through the power of the Holy Spirit we take part in Christ's Passion by dying to sin, and in his Resurrection by being born to a new life; we are members of his Body which is the Church, branches grafted onto the vine which is himself. . . .
>
> The first work of the grace of the Holy Spirit is conversion, effecting justification in accordance with Jesus' proclamation at the beginning of the Gospel: "Repent, for the kingdom of heaven is at hand." Moved by grace, man turns toward God and away from sin, thus accepting forgiveness and righteousness from on high. "Justification is not only the remission of sins, but also the sanctification and renewal of the interior man.". . .
>
> Justification establishes cooperation between God's grace and man's freedom. On man's part it is expressed by the assent of faith to the Word of God, which invites him to conversion, and in the cooperation of charity with the prompting of the Holy Spirit who precedes and preserves his assent. . . . The Holy Spirit is the master of the interior life. By giving birth to the "inner man," justification entails the sanctification of his whole being. . . .
>
> The grace of Christ is the gratuitous gift that God makes to us of his own life, infused by the Holy Spirit into our soul to heal it of sin and to sanctify it. It is the sanctifying or deifying grace received in Baptism. It is in us the source of the work of sanctification (*Catechism of the Catholic Church*, 1987–89, 1993, 1995, 1999 [notes omitted]).

22. The following quotes are employed by Norman L. Geisler in his *Systematic Theology* (Grand Rapids: Baker Books, 2004), 3:289–91. However, for the sake of continuity between the two sets of quotes, I am using the versions of the Church Fathers found in the New Advent Catholic Website (http:// http://www.newadvent.org/fathers/), except for one that I take from the *Catechsim of the Catholic Church*. I chose Geisler's book because my endorsement of it appears on its back cover.

23. St. Irenaeus of Lyons, *Against Heresies*, Book 4.8.1 (AD 180–99), available at http://www.newadvent.org/fathers/0103408.htm (April 20, 2008).

24. St. Cyril of Jerusalem, *Catechetical Lectures*, 1.3, 4 (AD 350), available at http://www.newadvent.org/fathers/310101.htm (April 20, 2008).

25. St. John Chrysostom, *Homily 4 on Ephesians*, 8 (inter AD 392/397), http://www.newadvent.org/fathers/230104.htm (April 20, 2008).

26. St. John Chrysostom, *Homily 17 on Romans*, ver. 3 (inter AD 391), http://www.newadvent.org/fathers/210217.htm (April 20, 2008).

27. St. Augustine of Hippo, *On the Spirit and the Letter* (AD 412), available at http://www.newadvent.org/fathers/1502.htm (April 20, 2008).

28. See Hilaire Belloc, *How the Reformation Happened* (Rockford, IL: Tan Books and Publishers, 1928), 1–37.

29. St. Irenaeus, *Against Heresies* 4.37.7 (AD 189), available at http://www.newadvent.org/fathers/0103437.htm (April 20, 2008).

30. St. Cyril of Jerusalem, *Catechetical Lectures*, 1.3.4 (AD 350), available at http://www.newadvent.org/fathers/310101.htm (April 20, 2008).

31. St. Cyril of Jerusalem, *Catech. myst.* 5.9.10, p. 33, 1116–17, as quoted in the *Catechism of the Catholic Church*, 1371.

32. St. John Chrysostom, *Homily 41 on 1 Corinthians*, 8 (AD 392), available at http://www.newadvent.org/fathers/220141.htm (April 20, 2008).

33. St. John Chrysostom, *Homily 3 on Philippians* (AD 398/404), available at http://www.newadvent.org/fathers/230200.htm (April 20, 2008).

34. St. Augustine of Hippo, *On Man's Perfection in Righteousness*, 20 [43] (AD 415), available at http://www.newadvent.org/fathers/1504.htm (April 20, 2008) (citation omitted).

35. As a Baptist colleague of mine said in an email to me in May 2008: "[M]any things essential to Christian belief and practice are not mentioned in Scripture—for example, prohibitions of euthanasia, abortion, pedophilia, necrophilia. Hence [is] the wisdom of the Catholic Church in regarding Tradition, not as a contradiction but as an extension of Scripture[, such as] in its formulation of the doctrine of the Trinity, the two natures of Christ, etc. Purgatory is therefore to be understood as an extension of the biblical doctrine of sanctification, for no one is permitted (or would want) to enter God's presence without being fully cleansed of all sin and thus to be fully sanctified."

36. The *Catechism* reads:

> All who die in God's grace and friendship, but still imperfectly purified, are indeed assured of their eternal salvation; but after death they undergo purification, so as to achieve the holiness necessary to enter the joy of heaven.

> The Church gives the name Purgatory to this final purification of the elect, which is entirely different from the punishment of the damned. The Church formulated her doctrine of faith on Purgatory especially at the Councils of Florence and Trent. The tradition of the Church, by reference to certain texts of Scripture, speaks of a cleansing fire [Cf. 1 Cor 3:15; 1 Pet 1:7]. . . .

> This teaching is also based on the practice of prayer for the dead, already mentioned in Sacred Scripture: "Therefore [Judas Maccabeus] made atonement for the dead, that they might be delivered from their sin" [2 Macc 12:46]. From the beginning the Church has honored the memory of the dead and offered

prayers in suffrage for them, above all the Eucharistic sacrifice, so that, thus purified, they may attain the beatific vision of God. . . .

The Church also commends almsgiving, indulgences, and works of penance undertaken on behalf of the dead . . . (*Catechism of the Catholic Church*, 1030–32 [some notes omitted]).

37. One finds prayers for the dead inscribed in the catacombs (first through fourth centuries), in the earliest liturgies, as well as in the works of many early Christian writers dating back to the mid second century. (See P. J. Toner, "Prayers for the Dead," transcribed by Michael T. Barrett, *The Catholic Encyclopedia, Volume IV* [New York: Robert Appleton Company, 1908], available at http://www.newadvent.org/cathen/04653a.htm [April 21, 2008].) According to Robert Louis Wilken, "Early in the church's history Christians gathered at the tombs of martyrs to pray and celebrate the Eucharist. The faithful of one generation were united to the faithful of former times, not by a set of ideas or teachings (though this was assumed), but by the community that remembered their names. . . . The communion of the saints was a living presence in every celebration of the Eucharist" (*The Spirit of Early Christian Thought: Seeking the Face of God* [New Haven: Yale University Press, 2003], 46).

38. Wilken, *The Spirit of Early Christian Thought*, 45, 47. From *The Catholic Encyclopedia*:

The testimony of the early liturgies is in harmony with that of the monuments. Without touching the subject of the various liturgies we possess, without even enumerating and citing them singly, it is enough to say here that all without exception—Nestorian and Monophysite as well as Catholic, those in Syriac, Armenian, and Coptic as well as those in Greek and Latin—contain the commemoration of the faithful departed in the Mass, with a prayer for peace, light, refreshment and the like, and in many cases expressly for the remission of sins and the effacement of sinful stains. The following, from the Syriac Liturgy of St James, may be quoted as a typical example: "we commemorate all the faithful dead who have died in the true faith. . . . We ask, we entreat, we pray Christ our God, who took their souls and spirits to Himself, that by His many compassions He will make them worthy of the pardon of their faults and the remission of their sins" (notes omitted) (Toner, "Prayers for the Dead").

39. *Catechism of the Catholic Church*, 2008 (emphasis in original).

40. From the Canons of the Council of Orange:

CANON 1. If anyone denies that it is the whole man, that is, both body and soul, that was "changed for the worse" through the offense of Adam's sin, but believes that the freedom of the soul remains unimpaired and that only the body is subject to corruption, he is deceived by the error of Pelagius and contradicts the scripture. . . .

CANON 4. If anyone maintains that God awaits our will to be cleansed from sin, but does not confess that even *our will to be cleansed comes to us through the infusion and working of the Holy Spirit*, he resists the Holy Spirit himself who says through Solomon, "The will is prepared by the Lord" (Prov. 8:35, LXX), and the salutary word of the Apostle, "For God is at work in you, both to will and to work for his good pleasure" (Phil. 2:13).

Canon 5. If anyone says that not only the increase of faith but also its beginning and the very desire for faith, by which we believe in Him who justifies the ungodly and comes to the *regeneration of holy baptism—if anyone says that this belongs to us by nature and not by a gift of grace, that is, by the inspiration of the Holy Spirit amending our will and turning it from unbelief to faith and from godlessness to godliness, it is proof that he is opposed to the teaching of the Apostles. . . .*

Canon 24. Concerning the branches of the vine. *The branches on the vine do not give life to the vine, but receive life from it; thus the vine is related to its branches in such a way that it supplies them with what they need to live, and does not take this from them. Thus it is to the advantage of the disciples, not Christ, both to have Christ abiding in them and to abide in Christ. For if the vine is cut down another can shoot up from the live root; but one who is cut off from the vine cannot live without the root* (John 15:5ff). . . .

Conclusion. . . . According to the catholic faith *we also believe that after grace has been received through baptism, all baptized persons have the ability and responsibility, if they desire to labor faithfully, to perform with the aid and cooperation of Christ what is of essential importance in regard to the salvation of their soul.* We not only do not believe that any are foreordained to evil by the power of God, but even state with utter abhorrence that if there are those who want to believe so evil a thing, they are anathema. We also believe and confess to our benefit that in every good work it is not we who take the initiative and are then assisted through the mercy of God, but God himself first inspires in us both faith in him and love for him without any previous good works of our own that deserve reward, so that we may both faithfully seek the sacrament of baptism, and after baptism be able by his help to do what is pleasing to him. We must therefore most evidently believe that the praiseworthy faith of the thief whom the Lord called to his home in paradise, and of Cornelius the centurion, to whom the angel of the Lord was sent, and of Zacchaeus, who was worthy to receive the Lord himself, was not a natural endowment but a gift of God's kindness.

(http://www.reformed.org/documents/canons_of_orange.html [April 23, 2008] [emphasis added])

41. Ibid., Canon 20.

42. Geisler, for example, writes that "Catholicism's overreaction to Luther obfuscated the purity and clarity of the gospel and conflicted with their own earlier Council of Orange (529), which denied semi-Pelagianism" (Geisler, *Systematic Theology*, 3:267). See also R. C. Sproul, "The Pelagian Captivity of the Church," *Modern Reformation* 10, no. 3 (May/June 2001), 22–23, 26–29.

43. For example, the teachings of Origen (ca. 185–ca. 254) were condemned as heretical at the Second Council of Constantinople (AD 553), available at http://www.newadvent.org/fathers/3812.htm (May 6, 2008).

44. "This is the meaning of the Church's affirmation that the sacraments act *ex opere operato* (literally: 'by the very fact of the action's being performed'), i.e., by virtue of the saving work of Christ, accomplished once for all. It follows that the sacrament is not wrought by the righteousness of either the celebrant or the recipient, but by the power of

God. From the moment that a sacrament is celebrated in accordance with the intention of the Church, the power of Christ and his Spirit acts in and through it, independently of the personal holiness of the minister. Nevertheless, the fruits of the sacraments also depend on the disposition of the one who receives them" (*Catechism of the Catholic Church*, 1128, quoting Thomas Aquinas, *STh* III, 68, 8 [note omitted]).

45. See Adrian Fortescue, *The Early Papacy to the Synod of Chalcedon in 451*, ed. Scott M. P. Reid, 3rd ed. (Southampton, UK: The Saint Austin Press, 1997).

Chapter 6 Every Word a Little Branch

1. Martin Luther, *Luther's Works, Vol. 54: Table Talk*, eds. Theodore G. Tappert and Helmut T. Lehmann (Minneapolis: Fortress Press, 1967), 165.

2. G. K. Chesterton, "The Romance of Rhyme" (1923), in *On Lying in Bed and Other Essays by G. K. Chesterton* (Calgary, AB: Bayeux Arts, 2000), 114.

3. I owe this illustration to my colleague in the Baylor philosophy department, Alexander Pruss.

4. Emphasis added in each scripture quote in paragraph.

5. Richard A. White, "Justification as Divine Sonship: Is 'Faith Alone' Justifiable?" in *Catholic For a Reason: Scripture and the Mystery of the Family of God*, ed. Scott Hahn and Leon J. Suprenant Jr. (Steubenville, OH: Emmaus Road Publishing, 1998), 104.

6. John Henry Cardinal Newman points out that scripture teaches us that God's declarations about a state of being do in fact correspond to actual states of being. See John Henry Cardinal Newman, *Lectures on the Doctrine of Justification,* 3rd ed. (Eugene, OR: Wipf and Stock Publishers, 2001; reprint of 1874 edition published by J. G. & F. Rivington), 81–82.

7. Emphasis added in each scripture quote in paragraph.

8. Emphasis added in each scripture quote in paragraph.

9. Emphases added in all the indented scripture quotes that follow.

10. See Norman L. Geisler, *Systematic Theology* (Grand Rapids: Baker Books, 2004), 3:258–64.

11. Paul A. Rainbow, *The Way of Salvation: The Role of Christian Obedience in Justification* (Waynesboro, GA: Paternoster Press, 2005), 222.

12. "James and Paul would be contradictory if they were speaking about the same thing, but there are many indications in the text that they are not. Paul is speaking about justification before God, while James is talking about justification before humans" (Norman L. Geisler and Thomas Howe, *When Critics Ask: A Popular Handbook on Bible Difficulties* [Wheaton: Victor Books, 1992], 527).

13. Rainbow, *The Way of Salvation*, 222.

14. As I noted in chapter 5, Peter J. Kreeft wrote something similar: "We do not do good works to get to heaven, but we do good works because heaven has gotten to us" (Peter J. Kreeft, *Catholic Christianity: A Complete Catechism of Catholic Beliefs Based on the* Catechism of the Catholic Church [San Francisco: Ignatius Press, 2001], 126).

15. "Our justification comes from the grace of God. Grace is favor, the free and undeserved help that God gives us to respond to his call to become children of God, adoptive sons, partakers of the divine nature and of eternal life" (*Catechism of the Catholic Church: Revised in Accordance With the Official Latin Text Promulgated by*

Pope John Paul II, 2nd ed. [Washington, DC: United States Conference of Catholic Bishops, 2000], 1996 [note omitted]).

16. Emphases added in all the indented scripture quotes that follow.

17. Robert C. Koons comments on this passage: "The saved are made perfect forever by Christ's sacrifice, but this perfection is also gradually realized through the process of sanctification. The two are inseparable: Christ has not made perfect (in eternity) those whom He is not now sanctifying (in time)" (Robert C. Koons, *A Lutheran's Case for Roman Catholicism* [unpublished manuscript, 2006], 88, available at http://www.utexas. edu/cola/depts/philosophy/faculty/koons/case_for_catholicism.pdf [May 9, 2008]).

18. Robert Louis Wilken, *The Spirit of Early Christian Thought: Seeking the Face of God* (New Haven: Yale University Press, 2003), xvii.

19. *Catechism of the Catholic Church*, 1989–92 (notes omitted).

20. Gregory Koukl, "Catholics, Protestants, & Justification," available at http:// www.str.org/site/News2?page=NewsArticle&id=5166 (Sept. 23, 2008).

21 *Catechism of the Catholic Church*, 614.

22. Ibid., 615, quoting Romans 5:19.

23. Ibid., 1992.

24. E. L. Mascall, *The Recovery of Unity: A Theological Approach* (London: Longmans, Green, and Co., 1958), 24–25.

25. See A. W. Pink, *The Sovereignty of God* (Grand Rapids: Baker Book House, 1984; originally published in 1919).

26. *Catechism of the Catholic Church*, 1993, 2008 (emphasis in original).

27. See J. N. D. Kelly, *Early Christian Doctrines*, rev. ed. (San Francisco: HarperOne, 1978), 189–220. Jaroslav Pelikan writes, "[I]t does seem 'express and clear' that no orthodox father of the second or third century of whom we have record either declared the presence of the body and blood of Christ in the Eucharist to be no more than symbolic (though Clement and Origen came close to doing so) or specified a process of substantial change by which the presence was effected (although Ignatius and Justin came close to doing so)" (Jaroslav Pelikan, *The Emergence of the Christian Tradition (100–600)*, vol. 1, *The Christian Tradition: A History of the Development of Doctrine* [Chicago: University of Chicago Press, 1971], 167).

28. See Kelly, *Early Christian Doctrines*, 189–220. See also Pelikan, *The Emergence of the Christian Tradition (100–600)*, 290–92.

29. See Kelly, *Early Christian Doctrines*, 189–220.

30. See Pelikan, *The Emergence of the Christian Tradition (100–600)*, 25, 59, 160–61.

31. See Kelly, *Early Christian Doctrines*, 189–220; and Adrian Fortescue, *The Early Papacy to the Synod of Chalcedon in 451*, 3rd ed., ed. Scott M. P. Reid (Southampton, UK: The Saint Austin Press, 1997).

32. See notes 35–38 in chapter 5.

33. See notes 35–38 in chapter 5, and Michael J. Taylor, SJ, *Purgatory* (Huntington, IN: Our Sunday Visitor, 1998).

34. See Craig A. Allert, *A High View of Scripture?: The Authority of the Bible and the Formation of the New Testament* (Grand Rapids: Baker Academic, 2007), 48–66. D. H. Williams writes: "The means by which the biblical books were regarded as inspired and divinely given for Christian doctrine and practice took place in the postapostolic centuries of the early church. This process was a gradual and untidy one that emerged out of the worship and liturgical practices of the early churches" (D. H.

Williams, *Evangelicals and Tradition: The Formative Influence of the Early Church* [Grand Rapids: Baker Academic, 2005], 55).

35. See Allert, *A High View of Scripture?*, 48–66; and Williams, *Evangelicals and Tradition*, 47–84.

Chapter 7 Evangelical and Catholic

1. Avery Dulles, SJ, "Evangelizing Theology," *First Things: A Journal of Religion, Culture, and Public Life* 61 (March 1996): 28.

2. J. I. Packer, "The Other Quadrilateral: What is Anglicanism?" *TheAnglicanPlanet. net* (November 2005), available at http://www.anglicanplanet.net/TAPEdible0511a. html (April 20, 2008).

3. Denny Burk and Ray Van Neste, "Inerrancy is Not Enough: A Proposal to Amend the Doctrinal Basis of The Evangelical Theological Society,"*Criswell Theological Review* n.s. 5/1 (Fall 2007), 69–80. See also Ray Van Neste, "The Glaring Inadequacy of the ETS Doctrinal Statement," *Southern Baptist Journal of Theology* 8, no. 4 (2004): 74–81.

4. Much of what follows comes from the ETS Website—http://www.etsjets.org (May 13, 2008)—supplemented by my own personal knowledge.

5. J. N. D. Kelly, *Early Christian Doctrines*, rev. ed. (San Francisco: HarperOne, 1978), 56.

6. See http://jimmyakin.typepad.com/defensor_fidei/other_christians/index.html (April 27, 2008).

7. Van Neste, "The Glaring Inadequacy of the ETS Doctrinal Statement."

8. ETS Bylaws, 12, available at https://www.etsjets.org/?q=about/bylaws (April 28, 2008).

9. *Chicago Statement on Biblical Inerrancy with Exposition* (1978), available at http://www.bible-researcher.com/chicago1.html (28 April 2008).

10. Kelly, *Early Christian Doctrine*, 53, 54.

11. Reformed theologian R. C. Sproul seems to concede as much: "Roman Catholics view the canon as an infallible collection of infallible books. Protestants view it as a fallible collection of infallible books. Rome believes the church was infallible when it determined which books belong in the New Testament. Protestants believe the church acted rightly and accurately in this process, but not infallibly" (R.C. Sproul, *What is Reformed Theology? Understanding the Basics* [Grand Rapids: Baker Books, 2005], 54). It seems that Sproul is claiming that the ecclesiastical body that determined (or discovered) the canon was not infallible but that its list of canonical books is in fact right and accurate (and by implication "inerrant"). That is a coherent position. For example, I am fallible, but I am able to issue inerrant statements, such as, "It is the case that I am fallible," "2 + 2 = 4," "The United States is in North America," and "All bachelors are unmarried males."

12. Burk and Van Neste, "Inerrancy is Not Enough," 71.

13. Strange as it may seem, the first half of the statement—"this written word of God consists of the 66 books of the Old and New Testaments"—is inconsistent with the second half—the Bible "is the supreme authority in all matters of belief and behavior." Here's why: if the 66 books are the supreme authority on matters of belief, and the canonical list of books is a belief, and one cannot find that list in any of the

books, would not that be a good reason to question whether one can limit scripture to that list of 66 books? In other words, because the *belief* that the Bible consists only of 66 books is a matter of belief not found in scripture, one could reject the first half of this statement based on the second.

14. Dogmatic Constitution on Divine Revelation, *Dei Verbum* (November 18, 1965), available at http://www.vatican.va/archive/hist_councils/ii_vatican_council/documents/vat-ii_const_19651118_dei-verbum_en.html (notes omitted).

15. First Vatican Council (1869–1870), Session 3, chapter 2, available at http://www.ewtn.com/library/COUNCILS/V1.htm#4 (July 21, 2008).

16. *Dei Verbum* 10 § 2, as quoted in *Catechism of the Catholic Church: Revised in Accordance With the Official Latin Text Promulgated by Pope John Paul II*, 2nd ed. (Washington, DC: United States Conference of Catholic Bishops, 2000), 86.

17. *"Read the Scripture Within "The Living Tradition of the Whole Church"* (ibid., 113 [emphasis in original]).

18. "Nestorianism . . . [is] the heresy which split the God-man into two distinct persons . . . [though] Nestorius himself indignantly repudiated this account of his teaching, and in recent times the whole question what in fact it amounted to has been opened afresh" (Kelly, *Early Christian Doctrines*, 311–12 [note omitted]). Nestorianism was condemned by the Council of Ephesus (AD 431), available at http://www.newadvent.org/fathers/3810.htm (April 26, 2008).

19. Monophysitism claimed that although Jesus was both God and man, he had one nature that was an admixture of both humanity and divinity. This was condemned as a heresy at the Council of Chalcedon (AD 451), available at http://www.newadvent.org/fathers/3811.htm (April 27, 2008).

20. Developed by the Catholic monk Pelagius (ca. 354–ca. 420/440), it affirms that human beings do not inherit Adam's sin (and thus, denies the doctrine of original sin) and by their free will may achieve salvation without God's grace. It was declared a heresy at the Council of Orange (AD 529).

21. Semi-Pelagianism maintains that a human being, though weakened by original sin, may make the initial act of will toward achieving salvation prior to receiving the necessary assistance of God's grace. It was declared a heresy at the Council of Orange (AD 529).

22. For example, Dr. John MacArthur, Pastor of Grace Bible Church, for years remained an ETS member in good standing while denying that the Second Person of the Trinity was eternally the Son of God. According to Pastor MacArthur, the Second Person only became "the Son" when he was incarnated as Jesus of Nazareth. He has since changed his views on this matter. (See Pastor John MacArthur, "Reexamining the Eternal Sonship of Christ," available at http://www.gty.org/Resources/Articles/593 [April 28, 2008].) He now conforms to the deliverances of the First Council of Nicea (AD 325), which had condemned the denial of Christ's eternal sonship nearly seventeen centuries ago.

23. St. Augustine, *On the Proceedings of Pelagius* (AD 417), available at http://www.newadvent.org/fathers/1505.htm (April 20, 2008).

24. St. Augustine, *On Christian Doctrine* (AD 397), 2.8.13, available at http://www.newadvent.org/fathers/12022.htm (April 19, 2008).

25. See, for example, St. Augustine, *On Baptism, Against the Donatists* 5.23.31 (AD 400), available at http://www.newadvent.org/fathers/14085.htm (April 19, 2008); and

Notes

St. Augustine, *Letter 54, to Januarius*, 1.1 (AD 400), available at http://www.newadvent.org/fathers/1102054.htm (April 9, 2008).

26. See St. Augustine, *Letter 53, to Generosus*, 1.2 (AD 400), available at http://www.newadvent.org/fathers/1102053.htm (April 19, 2008).

27. On the sacrament of baptism, see St. Augustine, *On Baptism, Against the Donatists* 1.12.20 (AD 400), available at http://www.newadvent.org/fathers/14081.htm (April 19, 2008). On the sacrament of confession and penance, see St. Augustine, *Sermon to Catechumens on the Creed*, 15, 16 (AD 395), trans. Rev. C. L. Cornish, available at http://www.newadvent.org/fathers/1307.htm (April 19, 2008).

28. See for example, St. Augustine, *Exposition on Psalm 99*, 8, available at http://www.newadvent.org/fathers/1801099.htm (April 20, 2008); and St. Augustine, *Exposition on Psalm 34*, 1, available at http://www.newadvent.org/fathers/1801034.htm (April 20, 2008).

29. See St. Augustine, *Sermon to Catechumens on the Creed*, 15, available at http://www.newadvent.org/fathers/1307.htm (April 19, 2008).

30. See St. Augustine, *On Man's Perfection in Righteousness*, 20.43 (AD 415), available at http://www.newadvent.org/fathers/1504.htm (April 20, 2008).

31. AAR Online Program Book for 2004 Annual Meeting, 20–23, November 2004 (San Antonio, Texas), available at http://www.aarweb.org/Meetings/Annual_Meeting/Past_and_Future_Meetings/2004/programbook.asp (April 28, 2008).

32. *Catechism of the Catholic Church*, 819, quoting *Lumen Gentium* 8 § 2 and *Unitatis Redintegratio* 3 § 2.

33. Ibid. (notes omitted)

34. John Henry Cardinal Newman, *Apologia Pro Vita Sua, Being a History of His Religious Opinions*, new ed. (New York: Longmans, Green, and Co., 1904; originally published in 1865), 147.